Hello God ... My Name Is Marc

Marc Taylor

Hello God ... My Name Is Marc

Published by Christ in You Evangelistic Association

Printed by Hiskey Ltd.

Scripture quotations are taken from the Holy Bible. Scripture taken from HOLY BIBLE, NEW INTERNATIONAL VERSION® NIV®. COPYRIGHT©1973, 1978, 1984, 2001 BY Biblica, Inc™

Used by permission of Biblica, Inc. ™ All rights reserved worldwide.

"NIV" and "New International Version" are trademarks registered in the united Sates Patent and Trademark Office of Biblica, Inc.

Scripture quotations taken from the King James Study Bible (previously published as The Liberty Annotated Study Bible and as The Annotated Study Bible, King James Version) Copyright 1988 by Liberty University

Scripture quotations taken from the Holy Bible, The Message Copyright© by Eugene H. Peterson 1993, 1994, 1995, 1996, 2000,2001, 2002. Used by permission of NavPress Publishing Group.

Lyrics of Stained Glass Masquerade. Written by Mark Hall and Nichole Nordeman. Recorded by Casting Crowns. Released 2005

Lyrics of Hear The Call Of The Kingdom. Written by Keith & Kristyn Getty

The author's royalties from this book will go toward the furtherance of the good news of the gospel of the Lord Jesus Christ.

CONTENTS

FOREWORD

Every now and again you meet someone and you think - there is something special about that guy! In today's evangelical "grey" society when we all tend to be politically correct, there arrives a guy who is different. In what way you ask - he is different because he is passionate about his Lord -passionate about people -passionate they encounter Jesus and yet fun to be with. He says clearly that we need Jesus not only as Saviour but also as a living Christ, as He by the Spirit energises and directs our whole lives and reveals Christ to a hurting world. Such a guy is Marc Taylor. Marc is different in that he is a man of destiny who just can't help leading people to Christ. Throughout Ireland, wherever he goes young and old find forgiveness and the new resurrection life of Christ.

Marc is an ordinary guy from Cookstown in Northern Ireland who tells his story - a journey of excitement, failure and discovery in which he relates very honestly how he discovered that the "good news" of the gospel is not only "getting out of hell into Heaven" but also about "getting God out of Heaven into us" and of how the Holy Spirit came to inhabit Marc Taylor and in a way changed an ordinary guy into an extraordinary guy and he encourages us to take this journey with him.

The challenge to us as readers comes vividly and powerfully in this book - the challenge of Galatians 2:20 - to die to our self and allow the risen life of Christ to live in and through us and add real purpose to our living.

I heard a comment recently that, God is good but He is dangerous and so I recommend this book with a spiritual health warning - Marc is good but he is dangerous - this book is good but it is dangerous! It may change your life forever as you ask yourself this question,

Can God use someone like me?

Norman Lynas

PREFACE

The lightning flashes and the thunder rolls as I sit in my little cabin which I use for study at the back of the church manse. I sit in awe at the Creator, the One who can, in an instant, turn a scene of serenity into a scene of intense noise and yet here I sit, His creature, the one who was formed in His own image (Genesis 1:27) and I can enjoy an intimate relationship with Him. I am overwhelmed at such a thought Francis Chan was right, there is no other way to explain it other than, 'Crazy Love'.

But yet, so often in my own spiritual journey with the Creator, it has been all too often one of failure and then repentance and so the ping pong continues failure, repentance, failure repentance. I constantly lifted books by great authors who were truly anointed by God for the very purpose to challenge and stir up my heart, men who had an encounter with the Holy Spirit of God, men who were without doubt instruments in the hands of Christ, but I could not just read one of those books and expect to have the carbon copy experiences these Godly men had. Men like, A.W. Tozer, Leonard Ravenhill, Dr. Neil Anderson, Jim Cymbala, Major Ian Thomas, Watchman Nee, Andrew Murray, Charles Finney, C.H Spurgeon and Billy Graham men who spoke so vibrantly on Revival, The Holy Spirit, Deliverance and Holiness. Yes I looked for, longed for what these writers had experienced but why was it that I still found myself more often than not crying from the depths of my soul, *What a wretched man I am! Who will rescue me from this body of death? (Romans 7:24).* In my experience in life I seemed to be a guy that more often than not had more issues than tissues. Where was it that the problem lay? Was I not reading enough of the Word of God? Did I not believe enough? The answer lay in one key thing, I needed to be desperate for God, it was to be Him and Him alone, nothing else or no one else could or should be taking His place. Somehow, at times I had perceived the Christian life to be sticking a 'Jesus Saves' badge in my lapel and shouting "Praise the Lord, I'm saved" and then living my life the way I saw fit to live it, squeezing in the odd great book I mentioned and longing for what these authors had experienced, reading a few chapters of the Bible and thinking that someday God is just going to zap me and that will be it, I will be just super spiritual in a flash. But the greatest radical, revolutionary preacher that ever lived said this, *"If anyone comes to me and does not hate his father and mother, his wife and children, his brothers and sisters – yes, even his own life – he cannot be my disciple" (Luke 14 :26)*. Yeshua, the Messiah, was not saying literally that we should hate our father, mother and families, of course not because that would be in direct violation to the command *"Honor your father and your mother, so that you may live long in the land the Lord your God is giving you (Exodus 20 :12)*. What Jesus is saying is that there is a distinct difference in being a 'Christian' and being a 'disciple', there is a cost, there has to be a cost to follow Him.

The purpose of this book is to be honest and open, to encourage and to tell of one man's story who, in spite of shipwrecks, disappointments, disillusionments and sin has learnt to claim the promises as recorded in the Word of God, *For Though a righteous man falls seven times, he rises again, (Proverbs 24:16)*. Stop hankering after sin, stop wallowing in self pity, stop carrying the chip on your shoulder, stop playing church and let us be desperate for God and passionate for souls. The question I of times asked myself was a big one, one that I had nearly accepted from the deceitful tactics of Satan that the answer was an emphatic, NO! Can God Use Me? Thank God, in His wondrous love and mercy He chooses to use 'damaged goods'. God always has and always will, Jesus said, *"You did not choose me, but I chose you and appointed you to go and bear fruit - fruit that will last" (John 15:16)*.

Blessings, Marc

CHAPTER ONE

BEGINNINGS

Proverbs 22:6 – Train a child in the way he should go, and when he is old he will not turn from it.

It is a warm, sunny afternoon and I am lying outside on the grass wishing so much that my dad had never asked Christ into his life 'Bible Billy', 'Bible bashers' are just two of the names that echo around amongst my friends in the housing estate in which I grew up. How I long to be eighteen years of age when I get to tell my family, "Sod off, that might be what you want but it certainly is not what I want." The boys who drink, smoke, party and have sex had a lifestyle that seemed way more appealing to me than a fellowship with no music, no apparent excitement and a dad who in my opinion has gone crazy in religion and has left the most exciting part of his life the bands, the booze and the banter behind him.

This is life, a Protestant housing estate where anything goes and anything that would be seen unusual in many people's eyes is usual in ours. I loved the hype of the twelfth of July, I loved the fact that we collected for the bonfire, I loved the sneaking away from my parent's sight to paint kerbs and write slogans on walls, to me this seemed what life was all about. My parents had given their lives to Jesus Christ, which is fine, but let me have my fun now.

Billy my father, well I suppose his name gives you some indication as to our family background. The Taylor family was a large family, we were a respectacle church going family, but no one in the family had a personal faith in the Lord Jesus Christ. The hub of the family was my grandmother May and grandfather Tommy. I have so many vivid memories of life as a very young boy, the Taylor's were known to be staunch Protestants and I guess this was impressed upon my young impressionable mind as a young boy. I recall on one occasion when several of the grandchildren were in our grandparents house how that granny May told us in a voice of authority that, "When you bleed your blood is orange, not red." (Thank God that both my grandfather and grandmother trusted Christ in their latter years of life and today they are both in the presence of the Saviour). From that point in my life there was what I can only describe as this battle raging in my mind. I had found a scrapbook belonging to my dad from his days growing up, there was much in this book about his past, his love for bands, a fervent love of booze and a clear picture of a man who quite simply loved the world. However, even though I wanted to twist and be contrary towards what he believed now, I could not for one second deny the change in his life. Yes, there was a huge part of me that wanted that 'old dad' back, but there was a small part that understood that only something or someone special could have changed him.

Sundays, oh no! That meant off in the 'Billy Bus' as my father was the driver for the local church to lift the kids for Sunday School hence they named the bus the 'Billy Bus'. We left at 9:40am for Sunday school at 10am for an hour, followed by the Lord's Table from 11:30am until 1pm or 1:15pm depending on how long winded the speaker was that morning, a quick rush home for dinner and then leaving again at 2:30pm for another Sunday School in the Blue Doors Hall from 3pm until 4pm, back home for a quick bite before leaving again at 5:50pm for the Gospel Service from 6:30pm until 7:30pm. As everyone else in the estate went away to the sea side for the day, or shopping, or just out playing football on the pitch right outside the front of our house, this was my Sunday and to me it was a millstone around my neck. So many times as I slumped down in the backseat of the car as it drove out of our avenue to go to church I was overcome with so many emotions, embarrassment of my mum sitting in the front decked in her Sunday finest and this hat sitting on her head, my dad with his Bible placed neatly on the dash of the car and anger as everyone else in the estate seemed to be literally standing laughing at the side of the road as we passed by. My family life was radically different to everyone else's in the estate and I loathed it.

How true it is when it says *Surely I was sinful at birth, sinful from the time my mother conceived me (Psalm 51:5).* There was not one person who had to teach me how to swear, or take a drag of a cigarette or steal tyres for the eleventh night bonfire, it came naturally to me because I was born that way. I had never understood the reality of when Paul said, *"The god of this age has blinded the minds of unbelievers, so that they cannot see the light of the gospel of the glory of Christ, who is the image of God" (2nd Corinthians 4:4).* How could I understand? I was one that did not believe and therefore was blinded by the god of this world, the devil.

But God is rich in mercy. Even though at Sunday School on numerous occasions we were scolded or moved into another class for being disruptive those faithful Sunday School teachers still sowed the seed and still prayed earnestly for us, consequently it was one of those Sunday School stories that was going to have a huge impact on my life and ultimately be used by God to bring me under sin conviction and lead me to repentance and faith in Christ. This story has had profound impact on many others who have read it or heard it...........

If a seagull was to come once every year to a beach near you and remove one tiny grain of sand each year to another place, by the time all of the grains of sand would be removed eternity would have only just begun. This challenged me and spoke to me on many different occasions, yet the devil and his demons are experts at what they do as they have had many years of experience at it and it is always the same line that he uses, "Wait, sure enjoy yourself first, you have plenty of time to become a Christian." What an old lie from the devil that he has used for countless generations, simply because it works, yet the Word of God is clear and life itself shows evidence of it, *Why, you do not even know what will happen tomorrow. What is your life? You are a mist that appears for a little while and then vanishes (James 4:14).*

There was a hymn in our church Hymn book, The Gospel Hymn Book, and it was Hymn 413, I literally took a cold sweat when I heard it announced as there were two emotions that welled up within me. The first was anger at the person who announced it and the second was the piercing pangs of conviction because in my current spiritual state I knew exactly where I would be spending eternity.

1. Eternity! Eternity!
Where will you spend Eternity?
This question comes to you and me!
Where will you spend Eternity?
Tell me, what shall your answer be—
Where will you spend Eternity?

2. Eternity! Eternity!
Where will you spend Eternity?
Many are choosing Christ today,
Turning from all their sins away;
Christ shall their blessed portion be:
Where will you spend Eternity?

3. Eternity! Eternity!
Where will you spend Eternity?
Leaving the strait and narrow way,
Going the downward road today,
What shall the final ending be—
Where will you spend Eternity?

4. Eternity! Eternity!
Where will you spend Eternity?
Turn, and believe this very hour,
Trust in the Saviour's grace and power:
Then shall your joyous answer be,
Saved through a long Eternity!

Procrastination, a process that is tactfully used time and time again by the devil and his demons. The devil will always induce the idea that there is plenty of time to become a Christian. One of the occasions that is paramount to me of when God spoke clearly took place at the age of 11. We had been given knives by some of the 'bigger boys' in the estate to make our way across Broadfields into a local Catholic housing estate and 'slash tyres'. Initially it seemed to me in my boyish mind that I was like some undercover special agent on a secret mission, however as the reality of the knife I carried was stabbed into the first car tyre a voice spoke loudly and the verse that I had learnt at Sunday School the previous Sunday hit hard, *There is no difference, for all have sinned and fall short of the glory of God (Romans 3:22-23).* Of course in Northern Ireland I was aware that there was a Protestant and Catholic divide but I had also the knowledge of how God viewed people, "No difference, all have sinned." Even in the midst of perpetrating such an act God spoke and the conviction of sin was real, the devil however whispered, "It is only guilt you are feeling, it will pass shortly, do not take this too seriously" and I believed that.

And so it was on a Sunday, one that I will never forget, a cold January evening in 1987, as a boy of twelve years old, I sat in the back seat of the gospel service that the story from Sunday School came vividly before me. I knew that eternity was an awful long time but trying somehow to get my head around this story to think of how long brought a shiver down my spine and a challenge to my heart as to where I was going to spend it. I left the service, went home silently, entered the house and went upstairs to my little front bedroom that I shared with my brother

Andrew. I started to try and pray, try and believe, had I enough belief, was I saying things right when all at once like a bolt out of the blue I started to sing a Sunday School chorus;

"There's a ladder to heaven for me,
There's a ladder to heaven for me,
It's Jesus the Saviour, who died on the tree,
He's a ladder to heaven for me."

It was then, right then that I realised that it was not about what I said, what I tried to do, how much I believed, it was not about the amount of faith that I needed to muster up, not at all, Jesus had done everything and all that I had to do was to climb onto the first rung of the ladder. In that very moment, in a simple childlike faith I took Jesus at His word when He said, *All that the Father gives me will come to me, and whoever comes to me I will never drive away (John 6:37).* What a thrill it was to know I was saved, I could not wait to tell my family, I could not wait to tell my friends, I thought within myself I was going to be a great preacher overnight. This whole thing was amazing. There was this fresh zeal, something that was bubbling over within that I could not explain at that very moment, but I know now as I look back over my life it was all 'piff with no punch'. How sadly mistaken I was to think that this journey was going to be always sunshine and never any rain. When Duncan Campbell prayed on one occasion with a group of students who seemed to be so full on and so energetic for Christ here is what he said, "Lord we need more steam going to the pistons and less steam coming out of the whistle." That was surely me in those early days. I wanted to shout it from the rooftops, I had no shame, no fear but sadly no realisation that even though I was saved I was now in the battle of my life. I had not realised why Paul had written, *Put on the full armor of God so that you can take your stand against the devil's schemes. For our struggle is not against flesh and blood, but against rulers, against authorities, against the powers of this dark world and against spiritual forces of evil in the heavenly realms. Therefore put on the full armor of God, so that when the day of evil comes, you may be able to stand your ground, and after you have done everything, to stand (Ephesians 6 vs.11-13).* Somehow, as I started to listen intently to the various preachers that I sat under in those early days of my Christian journey it seemed that I was being taught that the devil or his demons could not touch me now that I was saved and for years and years I never understood or had knowledge that the battle I was now in was a spiritual battle and a battle for the mind. So many evangelical Christians today still believe this and still teach this. Of course they will refer to the three enemies that we, as Christians face, the world, the flesh and the devil. Yes they will admit that the world can touch a believer and cause them to stumble, and the flesh will certainly cause them to trip up but not the devil, neither him nor his demonic forces can have an impact or come upon a Christian, how could he? After all a Christian is indwelt by the Holy Spirit of God so therefore it is impossible for the devil and his demons to wreak havoc in a Christians' life. Really? What utter nonsense! Let us be clear on one biblical truth, if the world can touch us and have an effect on us and the flesh can touch us and have an effect on us, then, be very sure that so can the devil and his demons. In those early days as a believer I was very sadly misinformed about the reality of demonic activity.

So it was that I went on my merry way thinking that now I am saved I have got to live and struggle and just hope that someday soon the Lord Jesus would take me out of this sinful world and take me to be with Him and enjoy Him forever. What a serious erroneous doctrine that is taught. Really I was no different than those Israelites who had been told by God that He wanted to bring them out of Egypt and into the Promised Land to enjoy the land flowing with milk and honey. For forty years many of them lived and died in the wilderness when they could have been in the Promised Land in approximately eleven days claiming God's promise, God's plan then is still the same plan today, **brought out to be brought in.** Later, in another chapter in the book we will look at this amazing truth that Christ wants you to enjoy Him now and then glory.

So, in those early years of my journey on the Christian path, I looked at so many believers and here they were and they seemed so holy. I revered these people and struggled to think that these people ever sinned so I adapted a similar lifestyle because I thought in my heart that this was genuinely it. I thought how I looked, what I wore, how I acted in church and the version of the Bible that I carried under my arm was the basis of this new Christian life. This 'comfy' Christianity and I guess a 'holier than thou attitude' seemed to be the thing to do. But all too often I was faced with hurdles, walls and obstacles that I could not get over and I felt so alone. Was there anyone that felt like me? Had anyone else struggles? Sadly in my case there was not one person on planet earth that I could talk to or be accountable to and even when I tried to talk to God I felt like David when he said, *How long, O Lord? Will you forget me forever? (Psalm 13:1).* I seemed as though I had to shout, "Hello God, my name is Marc, can you hear me?" It would do good I feel just to stop for a moment and take a Selah (a pause to think and meditate) and look at five of the things that new believers come up against.

1. <u>**Opposition –**</u>

I have mentioned this particular struggle first because I feel that this surely is one struggle that all believers will have at some point in their lives. Look at these following verses: *"If the world hates you, keep in mind that it hated me first. If you belonged to the world, it would love you as its own. As it is, you do not belong to the world, but I have chosen you out of the world. That is why the world hates you. Remember the word I spoke to you: 'No servant is greater than his master.' If they persecuted me, they will persecute you also. If they obeyed my teaching, they will obey yours also. They will treat you this way because of my name, for they do not know the One who sent me. If I had not come and spoken to them, they would not be guilty of sin. Now, however, they have no excuse for their sin. He who hates me hates my father as well. If I had not done among them what no one else did, they would not be guilty of sin. But now they have seen these miracles, and yet they have hated both me and my father. But this is to fulfil what is written in their Law: 'they hated me without a reason' (John 15 vs.18-25). Blessed are those who are persecuted because of righteousness, for theirs is the kingdom of heaven (Matthew 5:10). Jesus said, "Father, forgive them, for they do not know what they are doing" (Luke 23:34).* Opposition is sure to happen but you are in good company because Paul writes *In fact, everyone who wants to live a godly life in Christ Jesus will be persecuted (2ⁿᵈ Timothy 3:12).*

2. Temptation –

I know that when temptation is mentioned many people seem to automatically think that this is a 'man problem' but if you think that, then it has to be said that you are deceiving yourself. Look at these passages and see how real temptation is: *Now the serpent was more crafty than any of the wild animals the Lord God had made. He said to the woman, "Did God really say, 'You must not eat from any tree in the garden'?" The woman said to the serpent, "We may eat fruit from the trees in the garden, but God did say, 'You must not eat fruit from the tree that is in the middle of the garden, and you must not touch it, or you will die'." You will not surely die," the serpent said to the woman." (Genesis 3 vs.1-4).* The story that is found in the New Testament about two of the early church believers brings us face to face with the reality of temptation, *Now a man named Ananias, together with his wife Sapphira, also sold a piece of property. With his wife's full knowledge he kept back part of the money for himself, but brought the rest and put it at the apostles' feet. Then Peter said, "Ananias, how is it that Satan has so filled your heart that you have lied to the Holy Spirit and have kept for yourself some of the money you received for the land? And after it was sold, wasn't the money at your disposal? What made you think of doing such a thing? You have not lied to men but to God" (Acts 5 vs.1-4).* It is vitally important that we claim the Word of God which makes it clear on this very problem, *No temptation has seized you except what is common to man. And God is faithful; he will not let you be tempted beyond what you can bear. But when you are tempted, he will also provide a way out so that you can stand up under it. (1ˢᵗ Corinthians 10:13).* All of us struggle with temptation, in my own life I face it daily from many different areas. How sad it is that so often as Christians who preach and talk about forgiveness so passionately find it so strangely difficult to forgive a fellow Christian who has succumb to temptation. Paul wrote, *Brothers, if someone is caught in sin, you who are spiritual should restore him gently. But watch yourself, or you also may be tempted. Carry each other's burdens, and in this way you will fulfil the law of Christ (Galatians 6:1-12).*

3. Doubting –

I feel that one of the subtle ploys of the devil is to cause some believers to doubt. Now I have heard Bible scholars who I personally think ought to have known better say that "someone who doubts would need to go round the foundations and make sure they are truly born again," yet many Godly people in centuries past have struggled on many occasions with doubts. You see the devil plants the lie, then we take hold of the lie in our minds and before long we are in all sorts of mental and soul turmoil and the enemy has us believing that we are not saved at all. But take assurance from the scriptures,

I give them eternal life, and they shall never perish; no one can snatch them out of my hand (John10:28). For I am convinced that neither death nor life, neither angels nor demons, neither the present nor the future, nor any powers, neither height nor depth, nor anything else in all creation, will be able to separate us from the love of God that is in Christ Jesus our Lord (Romans 8:38-39). I write these things to you who believe in the name of the Son of God so that you may know that you have eternal life (1ˢᵗ John 5:13).

4. <u>Suffering</u> –

Suffering is something that Christians are not exempt from, the fact of the matter is that so often it makes us more susceptible to it. Yet while in the valley of suffering we can still have the option to trust in God that His way is perfect or let the devil get a foothold and sow that all too familiar lie of his again, "What sort of God is it that you have who allows this to happen?"

The scriptures give us plenty of verses and passages on this subject and here are just a few of them, *Not only so, but we also rejoice in our sufferings, because we know that suffering produces perseverance; perseverance, character; and character, hope (Romans 5:3- 4). Consider it pure joy, my brothers, whenever you face trials of many kinds, because you know that the testing of your faith develops perseverance (James 1 vs.2-3). In this you greatly rejoice, though now for a little while you may have had to suffer grief in all kinds of trials. These have come so that your faith – of greater worth than gold, which perishes even though refined by fire – may be proved genuine and may result in praise, glory and honor when Jesus Christ is revealed. Though you have not seen him, you love him; and even though you do not see him now, you believe in him and are filled with an in-expressible and glorious joy, for you are receiving the goal of your faith, the salvation of your souls (1ˢᵗ Peter 1 vs.6-9).*

5. <u>Devil</u> –

So many times we see that the world portrays the devil to be this fictional character in red tights with horns and having a tail and a pronged fork in his hand. When we perceive the devil to be like this it clouds our minds as to what the Bible clearly says about him.

Now the serpent was more crafty than any of the wild animals the Lord God had made, he said to the woman, "Did God really say, 'You must not eat from any tree in the garden'?" (Genesis 3:1). You belong to your father, the devil, and you want to carry out your father's desire. He was a murder from the beginning, not holding to the truth, for there is no truth in him. When he lies, he speaks his native language, for he is a liar and the father of lies (John 8:44). In order that Satan might not outwit us. For we are not unaware of his schemes (2ⁿᵈ Corinthians 2:11). The great dragon was hurled down – that ancient serpent called the devil, or Satan, who leads the whole world astray. He was hurled to the earth and, his angels with him (Revelation 12:9).

Though I have said to you not to under estimate the power of the devil yes he is mighty but you and I serve the Almighty and there are three attributes that God has that the devil has not:

<u>God is Omniscient</u>– God knows everything. There are so many times this thought kind of freaks me out, I have all too

often fooled my family, my friends and yes even my wife! But God knows everything! He knows our thought even before we process them, those things that I have done in which I was relieved that no one else knew, He knew! *Nothing in all creation is hidden from God's sight. Everything is uncovered and laid bare before the eyes of him to whom we must give an account (Hebrews 4:13).*

God is Omnipotent – God is all powerful. God spoke and it just happened, I lose the magnitude of this too often in my life. I think that there are times when God nearly needs to explain Himself to me as to why He did things a certain way or allows certain situations in life to go in a particular direction, yes of course there is no harm in asking, Why? But He is God, God owes me no explanation, God created us, we act as if we created Him, (sadly in many church circles we have created a certain God that fits our lifestyles). *"For my thoughts are not your thoughts, neither are your ways my ways," declares the Lord (Isaiah 55:8).*

God is Omnipresent – God is everywhere. Here we are as humans and we try to figure out God. I guess at times it can be quite frustrating to fully understand that God has always been here. We love to understand everything, but to understand God is in many respects trying to make God human. You and me are finite, God is infinite. David seemed to grasp something of the presence of God, *Where can I go from your Spirit? Where can I flee from your presence? If I go to the heavens you are there; if I make my bed in the depths, you are there. If I rise on the wings of the dawn, if I settle on the far side of the sea, even there your hand will guide me, your right hand will hold me fast (Psalm 139: 7-10).*

Here I was a new Christian on this new journey and I felt like I had to do this all on my own. How sadly misinformed I was, how isolated I had become and yet, unknown to me, the whole time God was looking a relationship with me and Christ, by His resurrected life, was saving me on a daily basis and longing for me to let Him in and surrender my life to His control. I was beginning to realise even in some small way that the Christian life is not for the fainthearted, this is a real journey with enormous challenges and the truth of what Christ had said was not just empty words but something that was to set the marker for those that heard the gospel, *"For many are invited, but few are chosen" (Matthew 22:14).*

Father, I thank You so much for Your amazing rescue plan that You put into place even before the world began. It blows my mind to try to even think that I was chosen before the world began. I praise You for who You are and what You are, I stand amazed at the love of God in sending Your only Son, the Lord Jesus Christ, to leave all that Heaven offered to come to this world to live as man but yet be eternally God. I thank Jesus for so willingly going to the cross to take my sin, guilt and shame, but most of all I thank You that on the third day Jesus Christ rose again from the dead and lives in the power of an endless life and wants to live in me. This is truly grace beyond words. I claim the promise by faith and I ask the Holy Spirit to lead me into all truth. Amen.

CHAPTER TWO

BACKSLIDING

Galatians 5:7 You were running a good race. Who cut in on you and kept you from obeying the truth?

Pressure, Porn, Puzzled, three things that very soon could have summed up my Christian life. The pressures of the housing estate in which I lived and the enticing fleshly things that my friends were involved in became more exciting, or so it seemed and very soon the love for mid-week prayer and Bible study had gone to be replaced by visiting a house in the estate to experience my first sexual encounters. It was here that I was introduced to the massive world of pornography, something that was going to take a hold on my life and further down my journey in life I would introduce it into our first family home. With the introduction to the world of pornography came the addiction of masturbation. The roundabout kept moving sin, confess, sin, confess, sin, confess and with it guilt, shame, bewilderment and the playacting on a Sunday. All too often I sat and if the lyrics of this Casting Crowns song had been written then I sure would have been singing them in full voice:

"Stained Glass Masquerade"

Is there anyone that fails
Is there anyone that falls
Am I the only one in church today feelin' so small

Cause when I take a look around
Everybody seems so strong
I know they'll soon discover
That I don't belong

So I tuck it all away, like everything's okay
If I make them all believe it, maybe I'll believe it too
So with a painted grin, I play the part again
So everyone will see me the way that I see them

Are we happy plastic people
Under shiny plastic steeples
With walls around our weakness
And smiles to hide our pain

But if the invitation's open
To every heart that has been broken
Maybe then we close the curtain
On our stained glass masquerade

Is there anyone who's been there
Are there any hands to raise
Am I the only one who's traded
In the altar for a stage

The performance is convincing
And we know every line by heart
Only when no one is watching
Can we really fall apart

But would it set me free
If I dared to let you see
The truth behind the person
That you imagine me to be

Would your arms be open
Or would you walk away
Would the love of Jesus
Be enough to make you stay

Was I the only one battling? Was there such a thing as sinless perfection? Could I experience God in a way that I never thought possible? All of these questions sent me into whirlpools in my mind but I seemed trapped, going nowhere spiritually and now the only thing that I really understood was what I used to hear the old time preachers saying, "Sin will take you further than you want to go, it will cost you more than you are willing to pay and keep you longer than you intended to stay."

This franticly paced, false picture of the Christian life continued for many years, I struggled so much with 'secret sin' but within me I knew that, what I thought was 'secret sin' on earth was in fact 'open talk' in Heaven. Many Sundays I went and shared my 'testimony' in many different churches, I had all the phraseology right and spoke on things that I knew the people in the particular churches liked to hear, but it was far from the reality of the life I was living. Pretending can only work for a period of time before truth takes over.

The spiritual rollercoaster was to continue and soon I met a girl called Heather. It was not very long before I realised that Heather came from a troubled family background, a dad and mum divorced and a mother who had attempted suicide on many different occasions. Heather needed me and, quite frankly, right then I needed her. The thing that was far from our minds at this stage was God, church or anything to do with Christianity. The reality was that with Heather's mum being admitted for long periods into a psychiatric hospital it opened the door to ongoing opportunities for me to stay down in her house most weekends and withdraw myself from putting on the 'church face' back home.

Then came a big shock to the system as I experienced the attack of other 'Christians' on my family, those we had thought were so holy that they could not sin, people who professed that they 'held the truth' but how is it that they had become backbiters, nasty, cruel and many times so unspiritual? For me, this was just the excuse I needed to get away from it all, after all why would I want to have 'fellowship' with people that criticised, slandered and walked to the opposite side of the street. 'Hypocrites' was the first thing that came to my vulnerable, struggling perception of the Christian life. Maybe the best life is the life in the world, the devil was beginning to sow his seeds of lies and, sadly, I was beginning to embrace them wholeheartedly.

What I needed now was a good blow out to get away from it all and so it was to Spain that I set out to party and clear my mind of the false Christianity I had observed back home. I finished my relationship with Heather and tried to start a 'new life' somewhere else. It was not too long after I arrived in Spain that I set out on massive drinking binges and everything that is associated with them. Maybe some readers think as they read this, that guy was not saved at all, I suggest that you read this verse carefully, *So, if you think you are standing firm, be careful that you don't fall! (1ˢᵗ Corinthians 10:12).* This was the effect of a wrong perception of Christ, a wrong doctrine on what it meant to be a real Christian and a wrong focus on what really mattered. Some Christians let you down – Fact – but what reason or excuse does that give us to run away or try to escape from the love of Christ and His ownership of our lives as Christians?

One night as I sat in Spin nightclub in Spain completely intoxicated, a dear man I had befriended from the South of Ireland was sitting with me and he said "Tell me something about yourself Marc" to which in my drunken state I replied, "I'm a born again Christian." His reply pierced me like a dagger, "And you are sitting in here in a state like that." This was a guy who was brought up as a Catholic and yet he understood one thing that I did not obviously understand, Christians are supposed to be different.

I came home from Spain and even though for a period of time I felt my conscience probing and pricking, I went back to a life of sin and shame. I resumed my relationship with Heather and sadly every single sin that went with that. Where Heather lived in Moygashel opened up the door to having no one to tell us what to do, or point out our wrongs or preach at us. We could do as we pleased, and that is exactly how we lived, I introduced pornography into our lives and with it all the sexual activity and sin that is associated with that. In all my years of sitting under preaching the closest I got to hearing anything remotely about sex being spoken on publicly in church was, *Marriage should be honoured by all, and the marriage bed kept pure, for God will judge the adulterer and all the sexually immoral (Hebrews 13:4).* Of course that verse is true, but I was struggling, there was a hold, a bondage and something that was laying siege to my life, I was just hoping that I would meet someone who stopped pretending that everything in the Christian life was always good, all of the time, someone to break the taboo and stand up and speak out and declare, "I am struggling." Why is it that the church fails to address the issues and realities of sex? As soon as the word sex is mentioned from the pulpit so many Christians 'shut up shop' and feel deeply insulted that someone has actually used such a word. God created sex – Fact- and He created sex for two specific purposes, pleasure and procreation. There is no sin in addressing the issue of sex in our churches, the world is doing a great job of selling sex to us from every angle, what we need is people that are bold enough and willing enough to especially teach the younger Christians about sex and the temptation and the dangers associated with it. No one taught us!

It was not long before another shock was to come, Heather was pregnant. How are we going to tell our parents? Can we sink any lower? Is there any hope for us? Are we completely abandoned by God? So many Christians would say "Yes" to the last question and so many of them did. Thankfully the God of the Bible and the God I serve is the God of the second chance and yes sometimes even the third and fourth.

It is Christmas Eve night and Heather and I are up in my parents' house when, out of nowhere, my mum asks a very probing question that got right to the heart of our problem, "So Heather when are you due?" How was it mum knew as there was no visible signs? It was a mother's instinct, mum had sensed it. My father and mother were only too well aware of the cold, unspiritual state we were in. Our parents on both sides were truly amazing and their support was overwhelming. Many Christians also were supportive, although in some cases the story made the headlines in the 'Christian Weekly Gossip' with the all too familiar strapline, 'Another pair bites the dust, let's kick them when they are down'.

Heather and I had made plans to marry in late 1997, however the news that she was pregnant had brought a new take on these plans and so it was that we arranged our wedding for March 1997. With marriage came all the changes that accompany it but foremost in our minds was the arrival of our baby in six months time. The birth of our firstborn son Dillon was life changing. We were parents, we knew God in our hearts although distant from Him had blessed us with a perfectly healthy son and we were honoured. Surely now things had to be different in our lives? I had responsibilities, it was up to me to lead by example, but the hold of sin in my life was entangled deeper than I had even dared to imagine.

It would be good for us now to pause and have another Selah at this point to look at how clearly God's Word tells how the devil can suck you in and take you further and further away from the truth. You recall in chapter one how I pointed out that God's Word plainly says *"Let my People Go"* God wanted to bring them out of Egypt and bring them into His blessing but I think it is worth taking a look at how in scripture Pharaoh so clearly typifies the devil and how the devil operates.

God's plan has always been the same right from the beginning for his people

1. Salvation
2. Separation
3. Satisfaction.

A young man was enlisted in the army and was sent off to his regiment, he was a Christian and was very apprehensive as to how he was going to fit in. On his very first night in base he was assigned to his dorm with the 15 other soldiers who would be serving alongside him in his section. When it came evening all the other men began to smoke, drink, play cards and gamble, the young Christian got down on his knees as he did at home and began to talk to God in prayer. As the other men witnessed this they began to joke and jeer and some even threw beer cans at him. This became the norm night after night until one day the young man decided to speak to the army chaplain about what was going on. After hearing about the situation the army chaplain said, "I am going to give you some advice. You have to respect these other men, go away somewhere quietly on your own or wait until the lights are out, then talk to God in secret, compromise man, compromise and don't try and upset the other soldiers." The young soldier felt so let down and perturbed at this advice that the chaplain had given him. For weeks the chaplain didn't see the young soldier until one day they bumped into each other and the chaplain asked "Well, did you take my advice?" The young soldier replied, "I felt like a trapped animal and after the second night I went back to praying at the side of my bed as I normally do." "Oh that was a foolish thing to do," replied the chaplain "and what happened to you?" The young soldier replied "Well we now have a prayer meeting in our dorm every night, three of my dorm mates are saved as a result of honouring my Saviour and now we are praying for the rest."

Compromise, you give the devil an inch and he will take a mile, you let him in the back door and he will take over the whole house. That is why Peter wrote, **Be self-controlled and alert. Your enemy the devil prowls around like a roaring lion looking for someone to devour (1st Peter 5:8).** Paul could write, **And no wonder, for Satan himself masquerades as an angel of light (2nd**

Corinthians11:14). We are encouraged from the Word of God to resist the devil and he will flee from us. Let me point out four compromises that Pharaoh (Satan) will use to draw us back into the world:- Stay Put, Stay Pretty Close, Stay Partly, Stay Poor.

•   Stay Put – *Exodus 8 vs. 25 – "go sacrifice to your God in the land"*

Pharaoh wanted the people to stay in the land and worship. The devil tries the very same ploy and he whispers in a new Christian's ear, "Of course if you want to become a Christian that is fine but sure stay in the world, don't rock the boat, you have to be living in a real world, you can't be so extreme in your beliefs now that you have to do things different to the rest." But take a look at what Moses says, *"That would not be right. The sacrifices we offer the Lord our God would be detestable to the Egyptians. And if we offer sacrifices that are detestable in their eyes, will they not stone us? (Exodus 8:26).* How similar it is today. When we take our stand for Christ and things that are spiritual and say that there is one God and only one way to Heaven we are told in return by the world that there are many Gods and many ways to heaven. *Jesus answered, "I am the way and the truth and the life. No one comes to the Father except through me" (John 14:6).* You see, when you and I claim to be a Christian and try to live holy and Godly lives we are called fanatical, but when we claim to be Christians and continue to live in the world and still participate in worldly pursuits we are called hypocrites.

Let me refer you to these verses, *Do not be yoked together with unbelievers. For what do righteousness and wickedness have in common? Or what fellowship can light have with darkness? What harmony is there between Christ and Belial? What does a believer have in common with an unbeliever? What agreement is there between the temple of God and idols? For we are the temple of the living God. As God said: "I will live with them and walk among them, and I will be their God, and they will be my people." "Therefore come out from them and be separate, says the Lord. Touch no unclean thing and I will receive you (2ⁿᵈ Corinthians 6 vs.14-17).*

The world has three main things that they are obsessed about today

(a) Fame – Pilate loved Fame, look at what it says, *From then on, Pilate tried to set Jesus free, but the Jews kept shouting, "If you let this man go, you are no friend of Caesar. Anyone who claims to be a king opposes Caesar" (John 19:12).*

(b) Fortune – The Bible does not say that having money is a sin, it is the love of wanting more money that is sinful, when it becomes a god to us, *For the love of money is a root of all kinds of evil. Some people, eager for money, have wandered from the faith and pierced themselves with many grief's (1ˢᵗ Timothy 6:10).*

(c) Fun – The Prodigal Son wanted to get away from the fathers house and the restraints, he just wanted to have fun. *"Not long after that, the younger son got together all he had, set off for a distant country and there squandered his wealth in wild living (Luke 15:13).*

The devil is trying everything in his power to upset our minds and suck us into the world. Popular TV such as Big Brother, Who wants to be a Millionaire, Pop Idol, X-factor, Britain's Got Talent, I'm a Celebrity Get Me Out Of Here, all of these so called 'reality programmes' can in fact turn you away from reality. All are about false Fame, Fortune and Fun. The world says we are to get with it, God says we are to get out of it!! *Do not love the world or anything in the world. If anyone loves the world, the love of the Father is not in him (1ˢᵗ John 2:15).* The devil is whispering in your ear, "Stay Put live the way you are, be sensible now there is no need to go outside the world."

- Stay Pretty Close. - *Exodus 8:28 Pharaoh said, "I will let you go to offer sacrifices to the Lord your God in the desert, but you must not go very far. Now pray for me."*

If the devil does not succeed with his first ploy then he will not give up so easily. He will say, "That's ok now you can be a Christian but don't deny yourself a wee night out at a pub or club, sure what harm are you doing?" Two of my favourite films are 'Rob Roy' and 'Braveheart', they both tell how during the English and Scottish troubles, as the Northern counties of England pushed into the Southern counties of Scotland and the Southern counties of Scotland pushed into the Northern counties of England the people living in what is known as the 'border counties' between the two countries were always the ones that suffered worst. They were very rarely out of trouble. Why? Because they were stuck in the middle and getting it from both sides.

Saudi Arabia and The Yemen in 1998, Ethiopia and Eritrea in 1998, Poland and Czechoslovakia in 1919, it was always the people living on the borders during these conflicts who got hit the worst. You see being a border line Christian and living pretty close to the world will do two things to you, it will cause you Trouble and wreck your Testimony. Pharaoh was introducing a lovely new enticing tactic, have one foot in the world and the other in your faith.

A border line Christian just does not work, look at what the Bible says, *"No servant can serve two masters. Either he will hate one and love the other, or he will be devoted to the one and despise the other. You cannot serve both God and Money" (Luke 16:13). But if serving the Lord seems undesirable to you, then choose for yourselves this day whom you will serve, whether the gods your forefathers served beyond the River, or the gods of The Amorites, in whose land you are living. But as for me and my household, we will serve the Lord (Joshua 24:15).*

The story is told of the little girl who went to bed and while her mother was down stairs she heard an awful thud in the room above. Rushing upstairs to see what was the matter she found her little daughter climbing back into bed and when the mother asked what had happened the little girl replied, "I fell asleep too close to where I got in."

I wonder is that you, have you fallen asleep to close too where you got in? Maybe you got to the cross for salvation but that is as far as you have got. You are a cross gazer, you are no different than this little girl, you have fallen asleep too close to where you first got in and it will not be long until there is an almighty thump.

You need to get beyond the cross, you have to view a risen Christ, you must see an ascended Saviour and you have to experience the power of the Holy Spirit. If you remain at the cross and never understand that the life of Christ is in you right at the very moment of salvation to make you an effective witness, then sadly you will remain in defeat.

- Stay Partly - *Exodus 10 vs.8 - 11 Then Moses and Aaron were brought back to Pharaoh. "Go, worship the Lord your God," he said. "But just who will be going?" Moses answered, "We will go with our young and old, with our sons and daughters, and with our flocks and herds, because we are to celebrate a festival to the Lord." Pharaoh said, "The Lord be with you – if I let you go, along with your women and children! Clearly you are bent on evil. No! Have only the men go; and worship the Lord, since that's what you have been asking for." Then Moses and Aaron were driven out of Pharaoh's presence.*

Pharaoh was not giving up easily and neither does the devil. This time he tells the parents that they can go but he wanted the children to stay. There are those of us who have this unmistakable privilege of being parents, how are we bringing up our children? Have we children still in Egypt, still in bondage? Keep Praying!! As I travel around the country I meet so many parents who are heartbroken, I witness the hurt and the emotion written across their faces. They have children that are engrossed in the world and all the pleasures that it has to offer. Do not be deceived, the world is appealing and it seems to offer so much but what the world portrays to give is not satisfying. Every time I go on holiday I am amazed at how on every street corner there are those advertising for nightclubs and pubs. In stark contrast I very seldom see someone standing in these holiday resorts offering the people real life that alone can be found in Jesus Christ.

Pharaoh thought that if he could keep the children in Egypt then without doubt the parents would have to come back for them. What does the Word of God say to us parents today? *Train a child in the way he should go, and when he is old he will not turn from it (Proverbs 22:6). Fathers, do not exasperate your children; instead, bring them up in the training and instruction of the Lord (Ephesians 6:4). Fathers, do not embitter your children, or they will become discouraged (Colossians 3:21).* It is tough raising kids and we worry and wonder if we are doing it right and being a good example to them.

You may recall the story of the little boy whose mum and dad were entertaining the visiting speaker one Sunday. On the way home the mum and dad were discussing the morning service and were giving out about the speaker and saying how hard he was to listen to and that they did not think much of him. As they gathered around the table for dinner the dad looked towards the preacher and asked if he would give thanks for the food. The little boy piped up and said, "Dad I thought you said you were never going to ask him to speak again because he was nothing but an old blether." Let us be careful how we live and speak in front of the kids. I wonder have you a child that is deep in the world and you sit at weekends breaking your heart wondering if he or she are ever going to come home? Can I encourage you to keep praying that God might deliver your precious child from bondage.

I want to highlight something to the younger Christians. Do you notice that Moses wanted the young people to go out and worship with the older people? Young people, let us never think that the old are not to be mixed with. You need to worship with them, you need to gain experience from them. Yes certainly younger Christians need time to be together for fun and fellowship and to engage and interact with those who are going through what they are but it is important that the younger Christians spend time with the older Christians to be nurtured and feed, after all the older Christians have been there and experience is an invaluable teacher.

- Stay Poor - *Exodus 10:24 Then Pharaoh summoned Moses and said, "Go, worship the Lord. Even your women and children may go with you; only leave your flocks and herds behind."*

Pharaoh now knows that he is on the losing side but he is still not willing to give up without one last throw of the dice and his final compromise was that they could go but they had to let their possessions stay. What a lesson here. Always remember Christian, what we have down here is not our own, it is only lent to us. God, the Creator owns it all. Paul wrote, *Oh, the depths of the riches of the wisdom and knowledge of God! How unsearchable his judgements, and his paths beyond tracing out (Romans 11:33).* I wonder how we are using what God has given us? We are to give an account of our stewardship. Are we using our possessions to God's glory or are we squandering them on anything and everything else selfishly? Not only does the devil want to rob us of our material gain and use it foolishly, but more importantly he wants to rob us spiritually. I wonder if the devil is trying to get you to stay spiritually poor today? Do not let him. God says, "Let my people go" He wants you out completely. God has always had a called out, separated people and that has never changed.

Here is what Bobby Richardson former New York Yankee 2nd baseman stood up and prayed at an Athletes Christian Conference " **Dear God your will, nothing more, nothing less, nothing else Amen"** That is it Christian, Total Consecration!

Pharaoh (Satan) not only had me back in Egypt when I should have been in the Promised Land, but now with the scriptural role that I was to have as head of the house I was leading my wife and new son deeper into the world. The battle in my life was at times engulfing me, it seemed so much easier to go with the world, to be a Christian was too difficult. The realisation of God looking a people that were different was not something new, here it was right from the beginning of His word, I knew in my heart of hearts that being a Christian was going to take a 'real man' to step forward, was I willing to be that 'real man'? Being 'different' is not an easy thing. I read this story that gave me some encouragement.

Jackie Robinson was the first African American to play baseball in the major leagues. Breaking baseball's colour barrier, he faced hostile crowds in every stadium. While playing one day in his home stadium of Ebbets Field in Brooklyn, he committed an error. The fans began to jeer him. He stood at second base, humiliated, while the crowd booed. Then, without saying a word, shortstop Pee Wee Reese went over and stood next to Jackie. He put his arm around him and faced the crowd. Suddenly the fans grew quiet. Robinson later said that that arm around his shoulder saved his career. This is what I needed, someone just to put their arm around me and say, "Marc, it is ok, we all fail."

What was it going to take? So often I had read this verse, *because the Lord disciplines those he loves, and punishes everyone he accepts as a son (Hebrews 12:6).* We needed God to break through.

God, my heart is cold, my love is poor, my praise is shallow but yet within me I know that the love of God is unchanging. How easy it is for me to lose focus and concentrate on everyone else and their faults and their failures and lose sight of the fact that You alone are faultless, sinless and the only one that I should have my eyes fixed upon. You have searched me and known me, You alone know my thoughts afar off, I cry from the depths of my heart, speak to me, change me from the inside out, draw me back to my first love, I pray in Jesus name. Amen

CHAPTER THREE

BROKENNESS

Hebrews 12:5 "My son, do not make light of the Lord's discipline,
and do not lose heart when he rebukes you..."

It is another typical Sunday, a good lie in and then a good Sunday lunch carried in, in front of the television, to watch the omnibus editions of Hollyoaks, Eastenders and Coronation Street. This is the man who so passionately believed that a Sunday was a special day to meet with the family of God and ultimately meet with God Himself in collective worship. This is the man that at one time, thought he was going to convert the whole world but that seems so far away from where I am right now, but yet there is an inner longing and yearning to be back where I once was. So often I had heard of this term 'backsliding' and I was riddled with doubt as to whether there was such a 'scriptural term' I frantically searched the Bible and looked at situations and Bible characters who had turned away from God but I wanted something for me, just me, I wanted God.

I lifted a book entitled 'Hymns and their Writers' by Jack Strachan that I had received in 1993 as first prize from the little Gospel Hall Sunday School I attended. There was one hymn that I loved, when it was announced and my father 'pitched' the first line (as there was no musical complement) it was one hymn that spoke to me and made me pause and think about the heart of the person who had wrote it:

O for a closer walk with God,
A calm and heavenly frame,
A light to shine upon the road
That leads me to the Lamb!

Where is the blessedness I knew,
When first I saw the Lord?
Where is the soul refreshing view
Of Jesus and His Word?

What peaceful hours I once enjoyed!
How sweet their memory still!
But they have left an aching void
The world can never fill.

Return, O holy Dove, return,
Sweet messenger of rest!
I hate the sins that made Thee mourn
And drove Thee from my breast.

The dearest idol I have known,
Whate'er that idol be
Help me to tear it from Thy throne,
And worship only Thee.

So shall my walk be close with God,
Calm and serene my frame;
So purer light shall mark the road
That leads me to the Lamb.

What person would have composed such words? Someone with heart, meaning, passion and someone who, I felt was just like me, desperate for God. The writer had to be someone who mirrored by present spiritual state, this man was on a journey, one of failure, waywardness and longing to find hope.

William Cowper, born on 15th November, 1731, his parents died
when he was six years old and he was sent off to boarding school.
Bullied and beaten by his school mates, he became an isolated
and insecure young man. At eighteen, William began to study
law but because of his mental weakness he was not in a position
to pursue such a career, in 1754 he was called to the Bar and later
was to be nominated 'Clerkship of the Journals' in the House of
Lords, but his fears and insecurities prevented this and, as a result
he tried to take his own life. Following such an attempt William
was admitted to a mental hospital in St.Albans where he remained
for almost two years. It was here that he found help mentally but,
more importantly it was here that he found the help he needed
spiritually and was saved at thirty years of age.

Here is what William himself said, "All that passed during these
eight months was conviction of sin and despair of mercy ...I
flung myself into a chair near a window and, seeing a Bible there,
ventured once more to apply to it for comfort and instruction.
The first verses I saw were in the third of Romans: *"Being
justified freely by His grace through the redemption that is
in Christ Jesus, whom God has set forth to be propitiation
through faith in His blood, to manifest His righteousness"*.
Immediately, I received strength to believe and the full beams of
the Sun of Righteousness shone upon me. I saw the sufficiency
of the atonement He had made, my pardon in His blood, and
the fullness and completeness of His justification. In a moment I
believed and received the gospel."

The Unwin family had brought him into their own home and
cared for him as their own son, but, sadly, all did not go well
for William Cowper. After the Death of Mr Morley Unwin,
Mrs Unwin, her daughter and William moved to Olney at the
invitation of John Newton. These two men befriended each
other and it was here that 'Olney Hymns' were penned by these
two wonderful men. However the dark clouds of depression
soon loomed large over William again and after soul turmoil for

months, at the end of his life he shouted, "I am not shut out of Heaven after all." On the 25th April 1800 William Cowper went to be with His Saviour.

As I read the words of this hymn, I was vividly brought back to that wee bedroom in 67 Millburn Close and I recalled so clearly that night when I stepped in childlike faith onto the first rung of the ladder but what had gone wrong? Surely I could not blame God? Surely I could not blame 'hypocritical Christians'? I knew enough of the Bible to know that I was accountable to God for myself just myself, I knew what Paul had written to the church at Corinth. *For we must all appear before the judgement seat of Christ, that each one may receive what is due him for the things done while in the body, whether good or bad. Since, then, we know what it is to fear the Lord, we try to persuade men. What we are is plain to God, and I hope it is also plain to your conscience (2nd Corinthians 5 vs.10-11).*

God had not left me, I had left Him and I needed to find Him. I lifted my Bible and cried, "God speak to me, show me please, do whatever it takes, I need You, I want to do something for You." I was oblivious to what I had just cried out, yes I meant it, yes it was what I wanted but I was unaware that saying, "......do whatever it takes, I need You" was a massive statement before God and something that God does not take lightly.

I opened my Bible and I went to one of my favourite childhood stories, I remember preachers who had preached sermons on 'Losing Jesus' and so I read, *When he was twelve years old, they went up to the Feast, according to the custom. After the Feast was over, while his parents were returning home, the boy Jesus stayed behind in Jerusalem, but they were unaware of it. Thinking he was in their company they travelled on for a day. Then they began looking for him among their relatives and friends. When they did not find him, they went back to Jerusalem to look for him. After three days they found him*

*in the temple courts, sitting among the teachers, listening to
them and asking them questions (Luke 2 vs.42-46).* I thought,
if His parents can lose Him then how much easier it is for me to
lose Him and not even fully understand how long it was since I
had lost Him. One thing became crystal clear to me, I needed to
do what His parents did, I had to return to the place where I left
Him. Vance Havner said, "It is one of the ironies of the ministry
that the very man who works in God's name is often hardest put
to find time for God. The parents of Jesus lost Him at church,
and they were not the last ones to lose Him there." This was
not going to be a quick fix. Yes I believed in the God of second
chances, yes I believed in a forgiving God but there was so much
bondage, there were so many things that I had got entangled
with, I needed not only to be restored to 'my first love' I needed
to be delivered and set free.

Monday the 19th January 1998, Manchester United versus
Southampton I had been eagerly anticipating the game all day,
but I was sick all day, something in my body was just not right,
I knew it, I felt it, but in my stubborn and selfish will in spite
of the best efforts of my wife I went out to my friend's house
to watch the match. Half-time, I was not enjoying the match, I
felt awful. I soon began to vomit before long pins and needles
engulfed my whole body and something seriously was going
wrong with my speech. I left the house and drove home and on
arriving in through the front door Heather knew something was
seriously wrong. I made it to the bathroom and bang, just like
that, no speech and completely paralysed I lay on the bathroom
floor. Heather frantically called the ambulance which arrived
along with my parents and I was rushed into the hospital. I
remember Dr. Hunter coming to examine me and then he called
Heather and my parents into the family room. I could see as I
lay on the bed my family broken, the news was not good, "Marc
is a seriously ill young man, the next few hours are critical."
A strange virus had attacked my bowel, it had rendered me
completely useless. I was moved to a room on my own where

the word 'Isolation' was placed on the door. I read the word, it summed up exactly how I felt, isolated. Day after day I looked at that word that was hanging on the door of the room, yes it was applying to the physical aspect of things but in my mind it was only describing my spiritual state. Hospitalisation gives you one major thing, thinking time. I had all the time in the world now to review my life, I was lying on my back and the only view that I had was looking up. If ever there was time to get my life into shape then surely it was now.

I recovered from that illness and was discharged from hospital, I knew the key to my recovery was the prayers of faithful Christians. I thought I was through the valley and out the other side but little did I realise that the emotional turmoil that I was going to endure for the next two years as a result of such a serious physical illness would be debilitating, horrible and very real. The first anxiety attack, heart racing, head spinning, sweaty hands, the feeling of the need to 'escape', was I going crazy? I soon realised I was not going crazy although this is how anxiety attacks make you feel. I realised in my heart of hearts this was a spiritual battle for my mind, you see that is why Paul emphasised that we need the full armour of God and especially protection for the mind, *And take the helmet of salvation... (Ephsians 6:17)*. That is it Christian, if the devil cannot have you and he can not if you are a genuine born again believer, well then he will not give up that easily. He will try to sow a lie in your mind that you will latch on to and believe and it will cripple you with fear and stop your effectiveness for Jesus Christ, he did it from the beginning with Eve and he is still doing it today, I have already quoted this verse but please get the importance of it, *You belong to your father, the devil, and you want to carry out your father's desire. He was a murderer from the beginning, not holding to the truth, for there is no truth in him. When he lies, he speaks his native language, for he is a liar and the father of lies (John 8:44).* There were days I could barely leave the house, going to church was a nightmare, and I had to daily force myself to work, the fear of even the normal things in life was overwhelming, the truth though was this, it was actually the fear of fear itself. I knew that it was not of God, how could it be, after all I was aware of this verse, *For God did not give us a spirit of timidity, but a spirit of power, of love and of self-discipline (2nd Timothy 1:7).*

I was broken, I was brought low, I was now in a place where I was beginning to be desperate for God, again I felt like David in Psalm 13, I was trying to get through and I just wanted God to pick up the line at the other end. Again I cried, "Hello God, my name is Marc, are you listening."

I think it would be good for us to have another Selah because maybe this is you, you are now where I was then. You are calling out and you just want an answer, let us look at someone in the Bible who found themselves in the same scenario.

Time and time again throughout my Christian life I have turned to Psalm 13. David had written this Psalm when it seems to me that he really is at wits end corner. He is just mentally and physically exhausted it seems that the problems he is facing with Saul are just relentless. There seems to be no end in sight and David really is crying from the depths of his heart, "Where are you God?" Many times he had been forced to his knees in desperation feeling in his soul that the Lord just was not listening to him anymore, many times he just wanted to hear the Lord answer him and this is one of those occasions. The bottom line is this, David is at a point where he cannot face another day, not even another hour, not even another minute, he is pleading to the Lord, "Please just answer me."

Many times in my life I have been here, many times in your life you may well have been here and no matter how hard you seem to try every day just seems as difficult as the day before and you plead with God to answer your cries. So many situations in our lives cause us to feel like this, maybe it is a work situation, maybe it is a relationship, maybe it is a wayward son or daughter but no matter what it is, you feel as if you are standing in David's shoes and you just want the Lord to answer.

It is when we are at the point of 'wit's end corner', when it seems that there is no way out, when it seems that we have almost given up hope of the Lord answering us, it is usually at that very point when the Lord begins to speak.

Too often it is so easy to seek a quick fix solution, too often I just want God to change the complicated situation but God, He wants to do something else, He does not want to change the Circumstances, He wants to change your Character.

I want to look at three very apparent stages in David's life under three corresponding titles that become apparent as I read Psalm 13, Disconnection, Desperation and Demonstration. I thank God so much when I read the book of Psalms for how honest and open David was about the situations that he faced in his life. When times were hard David did not hide behind a mask and pretend everything was just fine and rosy and there were never problems or he never 'brushed things under the carpet', David was a man that opened his heart and was honest with himself and honest with God.

- **DISCONNECTION** Psalm13 vs.1-2

   It is very important to note that in the very opening verses there are two different forms of speech that David uses. The first is what is known as the **erotesis** which means that you are asking a question without really waiting for or expecting an answer. The thing is, when my back is against the wall there are many occasions when I use the exact same figure of speech. Impatience is a wonderful thing, we are people who generally want an answer to something straight away, there is nothing as frustrating and could even get the blood boiling, than having to wait.

But look at the other form of speech that David uses, it is known as the **anaphora** which means repeating the same word at the beginning of successive sentences. The whole purpose of doing this, of course, is to emphasise something. You see, what David is saying, How long? How long? How long? How long? I am sure that we have all lifted the phone and tried to call someone and when you dial the phone number all you get is the engaged tone and you persist and keep on trying to make connection but it is to no avail. It used to be when the internet was on the go at the start, most families had the dial up connection, which meant that if they had only one phone line and they were on the internet and you tried to call, the line would be busy. This is how it seems to David, he is trying desperately to get through to God and it seems like the line is engaged and no matter how many times he redials to try and get through it just is not working. Notice two distinct things about David's Desperation in the first two verses:

(i) **A**lone – A horrible feeling to feel that you are alone. David seems to think that the Lord has forgotten about him. Do you ever notice in the good times when life seems to be all smooth sailing how time glides by? That familiar expression "time flies when you're having fun" really does seem to be true, but when life becomes more troublesome it is then hours seem like days, days seems like months and months seem like years and years seem like eternity and we start to cry "How long? How long? How long"? Can I take you to the place where the greatest feeling of being alone was ever felt? Come with me please to the foot of the hill called Olivet just about half a mile outside Jerusalem, here is a man, but not just any ordinary man, this is Jesus Christ and He is accompanied by three of His followers. The other eight are not with Him, one of His so called friends is away gathering up a band of soldiers to come and arrest Him. Jesus tells the three men with Him to "watch and pray" as He, Himself, walks on about a stones cast away which is known as the distance of death. He comes to the Garden of Gethsemane and prays. There is a verse and an expression at the start of the verse that really penetrates my heart every time I read it, *Going a little farther, he fell with his face to the ground and prayed, " My Father, if it is possible, may this cup be taken from me. Yet not as I will, but as you will"* *(Matthew 26:39).* You see, the Saviour went further than anyone ever could go because He was going to the cross. Sweat runs down His beautiful face, He groans in agony but the sad thing is that the three friends that He has brought with Him, Peter, James and John are all asleep, not even a friend comforted Him in this hour. The night rolls on and an angel comes to strengthen Him, He prays more earnestly, *And being in anguish, he prayed more earnestly, and his sweat was like drops of blood falling to the ground (Luke 22:44).* Jesus goes to His friends again and they are still fast asleep, He wakes them and pleads with them to pray, then Jesus moves away again and the Bible records for us that He prays the same words, *So he left them, and went away once more, and prayed the third time, saying the same thing (Matthew 26:44).* We have got to understand that it is not the thought of death that makes Christ sweat and groan, it is the thought of being left alone by His Father God that crushes His heart. It is the realisation that He is going to be left alone, uplifted between Heaven and earth to bear the sins of the world, to bear your sin and mine. Jesus goes a third time to seek out a friend surely one of the three would comfort Him in this hour of need but the Bible records for us this solemn statement, *When he came back, he again found them sleeping, because their eyes were heavy. They did not know what to say to him* (Mark *14:40).* Oh listen, when we find ourselves alone please always remember that our Great High Priest the Lord of glory, Jesus Christ, He knows only too well what we are going through, He has already been there. It is bad enough to feel forgotten and alone but David also feels he has been forsaken, "*how long wilt thou hide thy face from me?*"

(ii) Anxious – Look at the expression David uses in verse 2, *How long must I wrestle with my thoughts and every day have sorrow in my heart?* There are two things that are making David feel anxious:

    (a) His Emotions– If you have ever gone through any valley experience then you will know only too well what David is feeling, it is the butterflies in the stomach, you know that dull ache in the chest, when you go to eat you feel sick, the hands sweaty, the heart racing, no matter how we try to lift our minds on to something else it always seems that we end up back at the same place, the place of isolation, desperation, aloneness. This is how David is feeling.

    (b) His Enemies – David knew that God had promised him the throne of Israel but it seemed right now in the present situation that this was never going to happen. Saul was living a godless life and it seemed to David that he was getting away with it. It was greatly annoying David what his enemy was doing but it was more upsetting to him to see what the Lord was not doing. Unknown to David was this one fact, Saul may well have been a physical giant but David was in training to become a spiritual giant.

Do you ever feel like this? David was not the only one in the Bible who did. There were others. What about Jacob? You recall how he heard that Simeon was left hostage in Egypt but Jacob just gives up and announces that the whole thing is against him, *their father Jacob said to them, "You have deprived me of my children. Joseph is no more and Simeon is no more and now you want to take Benjamin. Everything is against me!"* (***Genesis 42:36***). But the reality was that, unknown to Jacob, God was working the whole situation out for him rather than against him.

- DESPERATION Psalm13 vs.3+4

If David is feeling the Disconnection in the first two verses, in the next two I can see something very evident in his life Desperation. David is not willing to let how he feels overtake him, no he is desperate and it is obvious that he is going to do three things:

(i) Keep **P**raying – David is in such a desperate situation that he feels he is about to die. But he prays and look at what he calls God, Jehovah my Elohim, Jehovah the God of **P**romise, Elohim the God of **P**ower. Do you ever get to that point when you are just longing for God? David is here and he will be here time and time again. Right throughout the book of Psalms David had to cry out to God, ***O God, you are my God, earnestly I seek you; my soul thirsts for you, my body longs for you, in a dry and weary land where there is no water (Psalm 63:1).*** There are times when we as Christians are so desperate we can do nothing else but cry but thank God He understands our tears. Time and time again throughout scripture you will notice that God allows His people to be brought to that place of desperation and when they cry out to Him, He will answer.

(ii) Keep **P**ersisting – It is so important to see that David's persistence is made in three requests. The first request is the word **"consider"** a word that is used in the King James Version, it really means **"look on me."** Do you get what David is meaning behind this? He feels that the Lord has somehow turned His face from him and he wants more than anything for the Lord to look at him and scrutinize him. But it does not just stop there he persists further with a second request, **"hear me."** David feels his prayers are going nowhere, sounds so familiar. In my life sometimes I am so like David I just want some kind of feedback just to know that God hears me. How often we feel that when we pray it is going no further than the ceiling above us? But David is not giving up without an answer, he persists even further with a third request and says *"lighten my eyes."* In other words *"give light to my eyes."* It is so easy when you become drained both mentally and physically to be discouraged in spiritual things but David persists and asks for strength. In Ezra's day the people asked for the same. *"But now, for a brief moment, the Lord our God has been gracious in leaving us a remnant and giving us a firm place in his sanctuary, and so our God gives light to our eyes and a little relief in our bondage (Ezra 9:8).*

(iii) Keep **P**ortraying – David is in a bad place and awful as he feels within himself there is still one thing that he wants above anything else and that is to portray the glory of God. The bottom line was that God had chosen David and Samuel had anointed him to be King. So if David failed in this, then it would be God that would be doubted. You see the little word **"moved"** in vs.4 that is used in the King James Version? It simply means **"to waver, to totter, to shake."** If David began to waver the enemies would ultimately gloat in the fact that God was unable to hold fast to His promises. Can I ask, when in difficult situations are we more worried about ourselves or are we worried about portraying the glory of God and making sure that His wonderful name is still uplifted?

- **D**EMONSTRATION Psalm 13 vs.5+6

It is wonderful to take note that David, although starting with Disconnection with God, and experiencing Desperation for God, ends with Demonstration of God's goodness. You will notice the word **'but'** that makes all the difference, how often there are situations in life that arise and then we can say **"but God."** So many times **"but God"** is written in scripture but I believe that the best one is, *"But God commendeth his love toward us, in that, while we were yet sinners, Christ died for us" (Romans 5:8).*

Have David's circumstances changed from verse 1 to verse 5 of Psalm 13? No, not at all but David is happy and content in one amazing truth, God has not changed either! Here are two things that David says God has demonstrated to him, please take special consideration that David is speaking in the past tense, **"he hath."**

(i) Demonstrates God's Salvation – The word is **"yeshuwah"** pronounced **"yesh-oo-aw,"** it is not just salvation in the sense of salvation from **S**in, or **S**elf or even **S**atan although all of this can be included, but this also includes salvation from **S**aul in other words the Situation that David has found himself in. Can we rejoice in salvation in all of these ways? Of course we can the Lord still saves you and me from, **S**in, from **S**elf and from **S**atan but never forget He can also save you from **S**ituations also.

(ii) Demonstrates God's Sustenance – the words **" dealt bountifully"** as recorded for us in the King James Version are actually one word in the original text, the word, **"gamal"** pronounced **"gaw-mal,"** it means to **"bestow, do good, reward."** You know what David really learns is this one truth, God has sustained me before and I know He will do it again. Was God's goodness going to be long lasting? Allow David to tell you himself, *"I* *was young and now I am old, yet I have never seen the righteous forsaken or their children begging bread" (Psalm37:25).*

This was it, I knew what was required. God was not ignoring me, there had to be some serious genuine repentance and it had to be from my heart. Sin is a heart matter *"The heart is deceitful above all things, And desperately wicked; Who can know it? (Jeremiah 17:9).* So if sin is a heart matter and it is then seeking God has to be a heart matter also, *And ye shall seek me, and find me, when ye shall search for me with all your heart (Jeremiah 29:13).*

Abba Father, I come to you in all my need, and my need is great, I am broken, desperate and I long to feel your presence again in my life. I claim Your promise that You never will leave me or forsake me and I confess before You that it is me that has left You. I feel so much like the Prodigal Son, I have left the love and fellowship of the Father's house for the far country, but it has robbed me and left me living among pigs. The blessings and the thrill that once were my experience and the joy seem a distant by-gone memory, but I need You, more than gold, silver or anything this world has to offer, I need You. Speak oh Lord, your bondservant is listening for Your voice. In Jesus name, Amen.

CHAPTER 4

BREAKTHROUGH

Psalm 51:10 Create in me a pure heart, O God, and renew a steadfast spirit within me.

"You are the man" that was the finger that was pointed correctly at David by Nathan the prophet, **Then Nathan said to David, "You are this man! This is what the Lord, the God of Israel says: 'I anointed you king over Israel, and I delivered you from the hand of Saul. I gave your master's house to you and your master's wives into your arms. I gave you the house of Israel and Judah, and if all this had been too little, I would have given you more....' (2Samuel 12:7-8).** There was no more need or time for me pointing the finger at anyone else around me, it was me, I was the man, God wanted to single me out and do something in me.

A Sunday afternoon, Heather and I sit in the living room of our house in Moygashel, things are strangely different, Heather is unusually quiet and to be fair so am I. I break the ice, "Heather," I say, "We need to stop messing about and we need to get right spiritually, we can't keep living like this." With tears in her eyes Heather replies, "That is what I want, I am so tired of this." BREAKTHROUGH!

We turn to Psalm 51 and we read it. I was well acquainted with the background of this story, David did what had pleased the Lord, but he had fallen and the fall was big. He had watched Bathsheba bath but that was not just enough for him, he had to have her and when he did the outcome was a child to another man's wife. The Bible records, *For David had done what was right in the eyes of the Lord and had not failed to keep any of the Lord's commands all the days of his life – except in the case of Uriah the Hittite (1Kings 15:5).* David had messed up, of course he had and messed up well, but yet when there is genuine brokenness and a heart that longs for restoration and renewal, God hears. David in a genuine state of repentance and brokenness penned Psalm 51; The Message version brings this out beautifully the feelings of his heart,

51 [1-3] **Generous in love—God, give grace!**
Huge in mercy—wipe out my bad record.
Scrub away my guilt,
soak out my sins in your laundry.
I know how bad I've been;
my sins are staring me down.

[4-6] **You're the One I've violated, and you've seen**
it all, seen the full extent of my evil.
You have all the facts before you;
whatever you decide about me is fair.
I've been out of step with you for a long time,
in the wrong since before I was born.
What you're after is truth from the inside out.
Enter me, then; conceive a new, true life.

[7-15] **Soak me in your laundry and I'll come out clean,**
scrub me and I'll have a snow-white life.
Tune me in to foot-tapping songs,
set these once-broken bones to dancing.
Don't look too close for blemishes,
give me a clean bill of health.
God, make a fresh start in me,

shape a Genesis week from the chaos of my life.
Don't throw me out with the trash,
or fail to breathe holiness in me.
Bring me back from gray exile,
put a fresh wind in my sails!
Give me a job teaching rebels your ways
so the lost can find their way home.
Commute my death sentence, God, my salvation God,
and I'll sing anthems to your life-giving ways.
Unbutton my lips, dear God;
I'll let loose with your praise.

16-17 Going through the motions doesn't please you,
a flawless performance is nothing to you.
I learned God-worship
when my pride was shattered.
Heart-shattered lives ready for love
don't for a moment escape God's notice.

18-19 Make Zion the place you delight in,
repair Jerusalem's broken-down walls.
Then you'll get real worship from us,
acts of worship small and large,
Including all the bulls
they can heave onto your altar!

This is the heartfelt cry of a man that is desperate for God, I can relate to this Psalm so much, Heather and I bow our heads and our hearts and we pray,

"Lord, we have messed up, and we know that it is against You and You only that we have sinned, we understand how we must have grieved Your very heart and we confess every single sinful thought, action, word and deed, some of which we have forgotten but they are all known to You. We want this clean heart that

David asked for, we want this right spirit, we want to serve You, love You and give You our all, wherever that may lead us and whatever that might take. Lord we are broken, we know that what we have said is heard by You, and we know that what we have said will carry a cost but Lord we are desperate for You. Please by the power of Your Spirit and by the scalpel in the Master Surgeon's hand do a work in us that only You can do, because we are fed up trying to do this ourselves. Cut away the fleshy pieces. We ask this in the name of Jesus, Amen.

As we opened our eyes and opened our hearts we knew that things would never and could never be the same again. But where do we go from here? No church or fellowship is going to be interested in 'damaged goods' after all that was the way that we were made feel, but "Hold On," the Lord said, "did you not just pray a heartfelt prayer of repentance and ask Me to use you?" Well of course we had. "Then trust me, take your hands off, stop being bitter, take the chip off your shoulder, you have some mighty lessons to learn and the Holy Spirit is going to teach you."

I felt liberated, excited and enthusiastic. I knew that if God could forgive David and use him, I knew that He could and would forgive us and use us. I was well aware while reading about the children of Israel's journey in claiming Canaan that the journey ahead was going to be that of 'valleys and mountains', it was going to be the very same for us but I knew the guide, the one that had led God's people in the past could and would still lead His children today. I knew that with Him nothing would be too hard for Him.

Is that you? Are you **B**roken, **B**ewildered and maybe even feel **B**eaten? I think another Selah would be good at this point, and let us look at the Bible and see how the Lord Jesus views people who are broken:

Those who have been Broken are those who have been Blessed.

I love this story in Mark 14. I am going to look at this story in the King James Version of scripture once more. It lets us get a glimpse of two very different sets of people, those who showed loathsome hatred for Jesus and Mary and a woman that showed Jesus nothing but love.

The word **"craft"** used in vs.1 is the word **"dolos'"** pronounced **"dol-os,"** it means **"to set a trap, to trick or to set bait to fraud someone."** These religious leaders are so angry with the Lord because He has thrown moneychangers out of the temple where these religious leaders were pocketing most of their profits. Now they want Christ dead because He is the One affecting their income. Sadly it is no different toady, 'religious people' and what I mean by that is those that have this 'pious Christianity' and want to set a trap or try and trip up other Christians. False holiness has not worked in the past and it certainly will not work in the present, God wants heartfelt people. There are three key things that are of so much practical importance to observe in this story

- **M**ARY and her **W**ORSHIP –

  What wonderful things I learnt from this dear woman as I sat and pondered all the accounts of this story recorded in the gospels, let me point out some things in relation to Mary and her Worship:

  (i) The **S**cene – When you read John chapter 12 vs.1 you notice that this event took place six days before Passover, which would mean that it took place on the Friday before the Triumphal entry. The name of the lady is not given in Mark's or Matthew's account but John in his account gives her name as Mary. This Mary of course is the sister of Maratha and Lazarus and you will remember that on all three occasions in the gospel records of her she is found sitting at the feet of Jesus. The place is Bethany situated on the Southern slope of Mount Olives, not very far from Jerusalem, itself. The house of course was that of Simon the leper who has been healed from his condition and is now putting on a meal to thank the Lord for what He has done, (do not get this confused with another anointing recorded for us in Luke chapter 7 in Simon the Pharisee's house this is different here). Jesus loved coming to Bethany, after all some of His dearest and best friends lived there, Mary, Martha and Lazarus. It is very significant to read in this passage and in other gospel accounts that the Lord Jesus enjoyed most fellowship, "as He sat at meat." Picture the scene here as Jesus sits at the table where most of the people love Him, they are His friends, He enjoys their company. Jesus Christ loved a fellowship lunch. Having fellowship over a meal or even a cup of tea after a church meeting is lovely, sadly many people do not like the idea of having a fellowship meal in the church building they see that as somewhat 'unholy'. My dear believer it is very spiritual and very scriptural. I love the fact that many churches have soup lunches and fellowship meals in the church what a way to make contacts within the local community, what an opportunity to share the love and compassion of Jesus Christ in a practical way.

(ii) The **S**cent - As Jesus sits at the table it is important to notice that this dear lady Mary comes to where He is, she has with her an **"alabaster box"** the word is **"alabastron"** pronounced **"al-ab-as-tron"** it is a **"perfume flask or vase."** In the vase or flask is this ointment called **'spikenard'**, an ointment that is very precious and she broke it. In the breaking of this flask two ancient eastern customs could be in view. Firstly in eastern custom if you had a distinguished guest in the home the glass that they had used at meal time would be broken after they had used it to make sure someone less distinguished could not use it again. Secondly when the body of a dead person was washed and anointed this flask would have been broken and the broken pieces were buried with the individual. Mary may well have had both of these things in her mind while doing so but the use of a little word **"on"** in verse 3 is so important. It is the word **"kata"** pronounced **"kat-ah"** and this word is important in the original because what it means is that when Mary poured the ointment on there is a suggestion that she was **"very thorough and gave more than beyond measure."** This ointment was a red-tinted ointment that came from an Indianan plant, it was purposely used in the embalming process and only the very wealthy of society could afford it. In John 12 vs.3 we read that Mary washes the Lord's feet with her hair but at the end of the verse it records this, **"the house was filled with the odour of the ointment."** Can you imagine the scent here as Mary poured the ointment out and poured it out beyond measure on the feet of Christ? The whole picture in view here is worship, there has to be something of fragrance in our worship. This is just not in reference to coming together on a Sunday or some other prearranged service, this is 24/7 worship. What scent arises from your heart during the week? Do we fill the house with a fragrant odour? What aroma do we create when we come collectively as a group of believers to worship in our fellowships?

(iii) The **S**urrender – Maybe you possibly think that Mary was showing off in doing this, I will put your mind at ease, Mary was in complete surrender to the Lord at this point. When she broke the flask she poured it on thoroughly, there was no half heartedness, it was all. This cost her and cost her dearly, it may well be that her entire life savings were in this flask but you see Jesus means more to her than anything she owns or has in life. Pride has gone here, self is gone, Mary is in complete surrender. After all, only prostitutes wore their hair down in public but here she is washing His feet with her hair. Only slaves washed the feet of others that is if slaves were available to do so, otherwise you washed your own feet but here Mary is surrendered and she is washing His feet. What a place of complete and utter surrender, Mary is going to worship and she does not care who sees her or who likes what she is doing, she is going to surrender her all. For many years I had this wonderful preconceived notion of what worship was. Anyone that raised their hands or swayed while they sang or prayed not in a certain way that I was used to, I thought that they were 'irreverent' or 'show offs'. Once again this was my perspective on how a Christian should look and should act, however this is a long way off what the Biblical picture is of surrendered worship.

(iv) The **S**earching – When I read this, time and time again I went over it and over it in my mind. Look at what the Lord says about Mary in vs.8, **"she hath done what she could,"** this really searched me. Is that what the Lord is saying about me? Is that what the Lord is saying about you? Can Jesus say, "They have done what they could." Folks am I holding back? I really think I am, I am not worshipping in spirit and truth really, the scriptures reiterates this, *"Yet a time is coming and has now come when the true worshipers will worship the Father in spirit and truth, for they are the kind of worshipers the Father seeks. God is spirit and his worshipers must worship in spirit and in truth" (John4:23-24).* The problem was I had changed the 'sprit and truth to a 'shirt and tie' I believed that how I looked was more holy in the sight of God than how I lived. When I look at my life I am holding back so much and I am only giving Him the leftovers when the whole time the Lord is saying, "I want first fruits." This dear lady, Mary, knew that before very long Jesus would be leaving her to die on a cross, she knew in her heart that she might not have another opportunity to give to Him her all. Can we grasp this just now? We believe and preach, "The Coming of the Lord draws nigh," but if we believed it with all of our hearts surely we would want to give Him more, give our all, do all that we could.

- MOANERS and their WAYWARDNESS –

Sometimes I have read Mark 14 and I have just hoped that it only contained the worship of Mary but the Bible records everything both good and bad. Sadly in this instance, there are also moaners and they do not like the Worship, they do not like the Way that Mary worships and they do not like the Worth placed upon her worship when she pours out the ointment. The reality is that the same kinds of people are still around today in our churches. Some believers actually feel that it should be the Lord who is thankful for the fact that we show up at church. Let me point out a few things in relation to the moaners and their waywardness.

(i) The Waste – There are two words in verse 4 that are very important, the first is the word **"indignation,"** it is the word **"aganakteo"** pronounced **"ag-an-ak-the-o"** and means **"to be sore displeased."** The second word is the word **"waste"** the word used is **"apoleia"** pronounced **"ap-o-li-a"** it means **"ruined, destroyed, perished."** These moaners in other words were actually saying, "We are not happy, what Mary has done with that ointment is an absolute disgrace its worth nothing now." It is important to note that in John's account of this story, Judas is the main spokesman, and the word **"waste"** that I have pointed out in Mark 14 is the exact same word used when it records in John 17 vs.12 the word **"perdition,"** this word is used about guess who? It is none other than Judas himself, how sad that Judas came down like a ton of bricks on Mary for so called **"waste"** of her money when Judas wasted his whole entire life and sold the Lord Jesus Christ out for thirty pieces of silver. You know what I have learnt? Sadly, many people are not worshipping because they are so conscious that there are those that would complain, how they do it, what they do, how they say it. Dear believer, what I want in my life seriously, above anything else is to be broken and spilled out, to shed tears in a meeting when broken and to lift my hands in praise while I am singing the sweet songs of Zion. Please understand it is not a waste when you pour out your heart in worship to the Lord, do not let the moaners discourage you.

(ii) The **W**orth – We read in vs.5 about the worth of the ointment which could have been sold for more than 300 denarii, approximately the annual income of a common worker. What worth do we place on our worship?

(iii) The **W**rong – We read in Mark that the poor are mentioned, but in John it records that it is actually Judas who suggests the ointment should have been sold and given to the poor. Sounds all very good, moral and proper to give to the poor but Judas in vs.6 of John 12 is called a thief. You know why he really is complaining? It is because he saw in this the possibility of a little cut for himself had he been given the ointment. Judas got it all wrong. Mary has a heart for giving, Judas has a heart for taking. Now I am not sure what you are going after today in your life, it could be a degree, a big house, a career or money. I have noticed in life when someone builds a mansion or rises to some sort of importance in society people will say, - "Boys he has done well for himself or herself," but when you get someone who wants to leave all and give their life to the Lord you know what people will say? - "Boys what a waste of a life there." I have learnt this myself that if you are not giving the Lord everything and first place in your life then you have sadly got it all wrong regarding what the true Christian life is about.

There is a beautiful illustration of worship that I have printed out in my study, it has spoken to my heart on so many occasions.

A sobbing little girl stood near a small church from which she had been turned away because it 'was too crowded.' "I can't go to Sunday School," she sobbed to the pastor as he walked by. Seeing her shabby, unkempt appearance, the pastor guessed the reason and, taking her by the hand, took her inside and found a place for her in the Sunday School class. The child was so touched that she went to bed that night thinking of the children who have no place to worship Jesus.

Some two years later, this child lay dead in one of the poor tenement buildings and the parents called for the kind-hearted pastor, who had befriended their daughter, to handle the final arrangements. As her body was being moved, a worn and crumpled purse was found which seemed to have been rummaged from some trash dump. Inside was found 57 cents and a note scribbled in childish handwriting which read, "This is to help build the little church bigger so more children can go to Sunday School."

For two years she had saved for this offering of love. When the pastor tearfully read that note, he knew instantly what he would do. Carrying this note and the cracked, red pocketbook to the pulpit, he told the story of her unselfish love and devotion. He challenged his deacons to get busy and raise enough money for the larger building.

But the story does not end there! A newspaper learned of the story and published it. It was read by a realtor who offered them a parcel of land worth many thousands of dollars. When told that the church could not pay so much, he offered it for 57 cents.

Church members made large subscriptions. Cheques came from far and wide. Within five years the little girl's gift had increased to $250,000.00 - a huge sum for that time (near the turn of the century). Her unselfish love had paid large dividends.

That caring Pastor was named Russell H. Conwell. He became the founder of what is now known as Temple University in Philadelphia, Pennsylvania. The little girl was named Hattie May Wiatt who died in 1886.

In a sermon on December 1, 1912, which honoured Hattie Dr Conwell reminded his congregation of the impact of that 57 cents –"Think of this large church," he wrote, "think of the membership added to it – over 5600 – since that time. Think of the institutions this church founded. Think of the Samaritan Hospital and the thousands of sick people that have been cured there, and the thousands of poor that are ministered to every year. Think of how in that Wiatt house (by which 54 cents of that 57 cents was used in the first payment) were begun the very first classes of the Temple College."

If God can do that with 57 cents think what He can do with $5.70, $57.00, $570.00, and even $5700.00. When we use the tool of treasure, of money, that God has provided us, and give, we don't give it to programs or buildings we give it to a cause – the cause of God.

True worship and love for Christ cannot be hyped up, it has to come from a heart that has been broken and a heart that wants to give.

• MESSIAH AND HIS WORDS –

I love what takes place here in this scene in Mark 14. When Jesus hears all that is being said about Mary He steps in, and from His words it is very evident that the Messiah has accepted the worship of Mary. Let us look at just four things:

(i) The **Beauty** – you recall how the men who moaned said that it was a waste. Well the Lord does not see it like that at all. He uses the word in vs.6 **"good"** it is the word **"kalos"** pronounced **"kal-os"** and simply means

"beautiful, fair and worthy." I am not sure as to what you are doing or how you are giving to the Lord. If you are giving from a thankful, overflowing, broken and spilled out heart then I want you to know the Lord finds beauty in it, no matter how small or how big you do something, if it is done for His glory then Christ views it as beautiful. After all we are supposed to be full of good works, that is one of the characteristics after salvation and not before, *But someone will say, "You have faith; I have deeds." Show me your faith without deeds, and I will show you my faith by what I do (James 2:18).*

(ii) The **B**asis – Jesus says in vs.7 *"For ye have the poor with you always, and whensoever ye will ye may do them good: but me ye have not always."* What the Lord is saying here is not the fact that it is not good to give to the poor, of course it is, but the basis He is laying is this, He is not going to be with them much longer, He is going to die for their sins, be buried, rise again and ascend back to Heaven, He is leaving them. Mary seized her moment to give Him her all, what about you and me, are we going to give all of our lives to everything and anything and just give Him part? This will never do the Lord Jesus Christ, He wants our all.

(iii) The **B**urial - When I read what Jesus says here, *"she is come aforehand to anoint my body to the burying"* the word **"aforehand"** is the word **"prolambano"** pronounced **"prol-am-ban-o"** it means **"to come in advance or before the time."** I sat and thought why are the rest of the disciples not anointing Jesus, you know why? Unbelief, you see time and time again Jesus had tried to tell the disciples that He is going to die, Mary on the other hand is just living her life in faith that what the Lord says is true, no need for unbelief. From this I learnt one important thing and it is this, even followers of Jesus Christ as close as the disciples can go with the flow and be carried along in the everyday activities without even grasping the very thing that the Lord is trying to tell them. How are we today when it comes to this matter of faith? Do we come in advance with our thankful hearts, our gratitude our worship and pour out to the Lord before something happens? Oh yes we come with our worship when something happens and rightly so that is an easy thing to do but let us learn from Mary to come aforehand.

(iv) The **B**lessing - Jesus finishes off speaking by telling all those present that this very act that Mary carried out will be for a memorial of her, the word **"memorial"** is the word **"mnemosunon"** pronounced **"mnay-mos-oo-non"** it means **"to put on record and never forget."** Jesus said that the worship of Mary would be told everywhere that the gospel would be preached, that was over 2,000 years ago and we are still proclaiming it today, what a blessing Mary of Bethany has been. I sometimes like to think that Jesus has a little Keep Sake Box and in it He has put some of the amazing things that He came across in His earthly ministry, the two mites the widow gave, this broken flask that Mary used, the gifts the wise men brought, the thanks of the one leper, the praise and thanks of people like the demonic man, the widow of Nain's son, Jarius's daughter, Zachaeaus and the thief on the cross. You recall that the "snuffboxes" in the Tabernacle held the wick that was burned out, none of them were disregarded you see because they were all part of worship and true worship cannot and will not be disregarded.

I wonder, are you broken and spilled out, is there a fragrance rising from you, have you, like Mary come to give your all or are you going to moan and hold a pity party for yourself? Oh to hear Messiahs words, "They have done what they could."

Supposing today were your last day on earth,
The last mile of the journey you've trod,
After all your struggles, how much are you worth?
How much could you take home to God?
Don't count as possessions your silver and gold,
For tomorrow you leave them behind.
And all that is yours to have and to hold
Are the blessings you've gave to mankind.
Just what have you done as you've journeyed along
That was really and truly worthwhile?
Do you feel you've done good and returned it for wrong?
Could you look o'er your life with a smile?

I am so very thankful that God chooses to use broken things, if He did not I would be on the garbage heap. *But God chose the foolish things of this world to shame the wise; God chose the weak things of this world to shame the strong. He chose the lowly things of this world and the despised things – and the things that are not – to nullify the things that are, so that no one may boast before him (1ˢᵗ Corinthians 1: 27-29).*

I had one massive problem in my life, in all honesty it is something that I still struggle with periodically and that is how people see me. This Bible story about Mary completely eradicates that problem, it is not about what people think and it is not about what they will say, the penultimate thing is this, how does God see me?

There is a wonderful story that is recorded in the book entitled, Praying the Lord's Prayer for Spiritual Breakthrough by Dr. Elmer Towns, it is a simple illustration but with such a profound message in it:

A small boy was playing with his french fries, dipping the end of one in the ketchup, and then waving it like a baton. His father was enjoying the moment. Mother had gone to a seminar, so for lunch the father took out his son and bought him a hamburger and french fries.

The young boy was more interested in playing with the french fries than eating them, though. "Eat your french fries..." the father coaxed. The son continued to wave his "french-fry baton," and the band played on. The father looked at his watch, but he did not have anywhere he had to be.

It was his habit to hurry about everything. After lunch, they were just going back home. Then almost by instinct, the father reached over and did something most fathers have done. He took one french fry out of his son's package.

"No!" the son said sharply, and slapped the father's hand. Then, raising his voice, he repeated, "No!" Apparently no one saw the little boy slap at his father's hand. No one heard what the little boy said.

The stunned father sat surveying the situation, though saying nothing. Who does he think he is? he thought. He's my son ...I bought these french fries, and I should be able to eat the fries that he won't eat!

That was not the case, though. The little boy had already gone back to leading his make-believe band as though he had forgotten the situation. The father, however, had not forgotten what happened. He thought to himself, I could get mad and never buy him another french fry in his life.

The father was not mad at his son, though; he was more surprised than anything. He was not the type to get even. If anything, he was a mild kind of guy. He continued to think. I could bury him in french fries and smother him in ketchup, I love him so much.

The father sat in the plastic chair, watching his son dip another fry in ketchup, and lead the band. The little guy had no idea of the thoughts going through his father's mind. We are like little children playing at life. Our heavenly Father reaches over to take

one of our french fries – say in the form of wanting a couple
of hours of worship on Sunday, or asking that we support His
Church with our money.

Too often we slap God's hand, telling Him, "No! Keep Your hand
out of my life."

God does not want to take all our french fries from us. He wants
just a taste. Like a selfish child, however, we say, "No!"

The question of the little boy and his father is a question about
our Heavenly Father and His children:

Who owns your french fries? When we are thankful to God we
recognize that it is God who owns our french fries. A thankful
heart makes room for God's plan and makes way for God's
provision!

Thank you God for breaking me, the fragrance can only smell
sweetest and strongest when the container is broken. Your ways
certainly are not our ways but I know and acknowledge that
God's ways are perfect. The Bible says that You came not to call
righteous people but sinners to repentance and that makes me
qualify. I have received the gift of salvation, but I want more. The
following, the leading, the fruitfulness and the filling. Take up
this broken vessel, because You are the potter and I am just the
clay and You alone are the only One who can mould it and make
it into something that is fit for the use of the Master. I humbly
plead for this in the beautiful name of Jesus, Amen.

CHAPTER FIVE

BLESSINGS

Ephesians 1:3 Praise be to the God and Father of our Lord Jesus Christ, who has blessed us in the heavenly realms with every spiritual blessing in Christ.

Finding your way back into the work of God after being distant from it for so long does not just happen overnight, nor should it. There ought to be that period of time that is spent back at the best school I know, 'The School of The Master'. There has to be a lot of chiselling and drilling and refining work to be wrought out. Not for one moment do we seek to receive the appraisal of men but we are to be good stewards in light of what God has blessed us with and it is during this time that we learn about the cultivating work of the Holy Spirit of God.

This lovely verse sparkled like a diamond as I read it, ***But when he, the Spirit of truth, comes, he will guide you into all truth (John 16:13).*** The Holy Spirit, is that not for those charismatic Christians I thought. Sadly, with my past theology and background I could count on the one hand how often I had heard sermons on the Holy Spirit. Yes, I was taught about the trinity, God the Father, God the Son and God the Holy Spirit. I had often heard messages on the Attributes and Holiness of God and so many times too I heard teaching on the Atoning, Redemptive and Vicarious work of the Lord Jesus Christ, all of which was necessary and totally true. But why was it that people were afraid to talk or preach about the Holy Spirit? Of course, the reality, is that conservative evangelicals try to play down the work of the

Holy Spirit while the charismatic movement tries to play up the work of the Holy Spirit but here I am and I want to be led by the Holy Spirit, I do not want to be another spat out, moulded believer from some theology of man, I want to be God's man, led by God, filled with the Holy Spirit and constantly open to the teaching of the Holy Spirit.

My inquisitive mind started to work overtime. I knew in my heart that what I had enjoyed before I wandered away from the Lord was real. I was saved of that I was sure, but yet, it seemed, that even then I was going through the motions, I had a limited view of what it meant to be a Christian, I loved reading this verse, *So if the Son sets you free, you will be free indeed (John 8:36)*. But yet, even though I knew I was free in Christ because I claimed that promise, it felt as if I was entangled with another bondage, it seemed that, although I was delivered from my sinful past, I was not experiencing the freedom that I should have had in Christ, the type of freedom that those early Christians had in the New Testament. But church as I know it is way different than that described in the New Testament, "but this was in the past" I was being told, but surely the God of the past was the God of the present? Vance Havner said, "The church is so subnormal that if it ever got back to the New Testament normal it would seem to be abnormal." Sadly, I had been led to believe that at Pentecost, the Gifts of the Spirit and the Power of the Holy Spirit were 'signs given to the early church' but how did that tie in with this verse, *And afterward I will pour out my Spirit on all people. Your sons and daughters will prophesy, your old men will dream dreams, your younger men will see visions. Even on my servants, both men and women, I will pour out my Spirit in those days (Joel 2:28-29).* Was that some past experience that I could not come into the good off and enjoy presently in my own Christian journey? Was I to read the scripture and covet what these people had and never experience it for myself? I had heard so often this verse quoted used in the defence to suggest that the gifts of the Spirit had ceased, *But when perfection comes, the imperfect disappears (1ˢᵗ Corinthians 13:10).* I was nearly convinced that what these people were saying this was in reference to "the complete cannon of Scripture" was the truth, but that is totally wrong. How could that be the case? The Holy Spirit came in power at Pentecost and I read of nowhere in scripture that says that He has finished the work He has been given to perform, has stopped now, or even changed in this church age. The answer is very simple, it is the church that has changed the operational work of the Holy Spirit is still the same.

I went back again to the children of Israel and how they had been delivered from Egypt and now thought it normal to be living in the wilderness, but yet the Word of God was saying something entirely different, *So I have come down to rescue them from the hand of the Egyptians and to bring them up out of that land into a good and spacious land, a land flowing with milk and honey .... (Exodus 3:8).* This is very clear cut, God wants to bring them out, to bring them in. But yet when you read the story of what happened you will soon discover that there were ten spies who told the people that they could not go in and claim the land and only two (Joshua and Caleb) who warned the people that God's instruction was to bring them out to bring them in. Sadly for the next forty years they wandered in a spiritual wilderness and as I have already mentioned in a previous chapter they could have claimed the promise and been in the land in eleven days.

This is me, that is where I have been, wandering about in a spiritual wilderness thinking that this is the Christian life and it can get no better while living in this world when the truth of the matter is that I should be enjoying Christ now.

Major W. Ian Thomas said, **"Everything that God is you have, you cannot have anymore, you need not have any less"**.

I did not want more, I did not want less, I wanted to claim what I had in Christ now. Maybe that is you, you are in some spiritual wilderness and you have been wandering there for some time and unless the Holy Spirit leads you 'into all truth' you could be wandering about there until the Lord comes or calls you. You do not need to, Christ wants you to enjoy Him now.

At this point I think we should have another Selah and look at some important, practical lessons from the Bible which may help. It is all very well praying for change and looking for a revival but before that blessing is to come, you and I have got to get the right perception of ourselves and a true perspective of God. There is no better book I think that gives us this in full meaning than Isaiah, take your time over these few verses because there is so much depth and practical teaching in them for us to learn in order to experience God's blessing. I would like to refer to these passages in the King James Version in order for us to lift out some great truths.

The voice of him that crieth in the wilderness, Prepare ye the way of the LORD, make straight in the desert a highway for our God. Every valley shall be exalted, and every mountain and hill shall be made low: and the crooked shall be made straight, and the rough places plain: And the glory of the LORD shall be revealed, and all flesh shall see it together: for the mouth of the LORD hath spoken it (Isaiah 40 vs.3-5).

For thus saith the high and lofty One that inhabiteth eternity, whose name is Holy; I dwell in the high and holy place, with him also that is of a contrite and humble spirit, to revive the spirit of the humble, and to revive the heart of the contrite ones (Isaiah 57:15).

Of course when you read Isaiah 40 vs.3, you will automatically see that the work of John the Baptist is being talked about here, how the way would be prepared for the revelation of God's glory in flesh to be made known and surely, in essence, that is the whole crux of the matter, we simply need God.

When I looked up the word **'highway'** in the dictionary it said, **"Thoroughfare to a higher level."** Is that not what we all need?

We need a through road to a higher level of spiritual living. We sing it so often,

"I'm pressing on the upward way,
New heights I'm gaining every day,
Still praying as I onward bound,
Lord plant my feet on higher ground.
Lord, lift me up and let me stand,
By faith, on heavens table land,
A higher plane than I have found,
Lord, plant my feet on higher ground."

Isaiah is simply giving the people instruction on how to get from one place to another, they need to get from the desert place to a higher place of revival. A highway will always take you from one place to your destination, and this is what this is all about we are really talking about getting from A to B. A is vs.3 and B is vs.5 but in between we have vs.4 and this is the place we must pass through if we are to enjoy the blessings of God. Revival, the cry of 21st century Christianity but yet the true meaning of revival has been lost. Brian Edwards in his book entitled 'revival' says, "A true Holy spirit revival is a remarkable increase in the spiritual life of a large number of God's people, accompanied by a awesome awareness of the presence of God, intensity of prayer and praise, a deep conviction of sin with a passionate longing for holiness and unusual effectiveness in evangelism, leading to the salvation of many unbelievers. Revival is remarkable, large, effective and, above all, it is something God brings about" (page 28-29). We cannot 'create' revival, something that is pre-planned and organised is in no way a true Heaven sent revival. Why is that we immediately associate the word revival with people who do not know Christ? They are dead spiritually, they cannot be revived what they need is life! Douglas Brown put it like this while preaching at Keswick Convention in 1922, "Revival is a church word; it has to do with God's people. You cannot revive the world; the world is dead in trespasses and sins' you cannot revive a corpse. But you can revitalize where there is life". So there is groundwork that needs to be carried out amongst the people of God first before God sends down revival. Let me show you four key things from verse 4 in order to explain to you how we are to experience blessing:

• THE **L**OWERING - "Every Valley "

We all know what a valley is, it simply means, '**a gorge, a dell, a basin, a low place.**' Isaiah says, *"With him also that is of a contrite and humble spirit, to revive the spirit of the humble, and to revive the heart of the contrite ones."* The very first thing that I have learnt about blessing is that we have got to be brought low in order to get a real true glimpse of who God is. I wonder is that you? You have been brought low, maybe you are reading this and you are in the very midst of the valley and you say to me, "Marc I really don't know if I could get any lower." It is so easy for us, as Christians, to bemoan our circumstances and situations, so often we pray, "Lord change my **C**ircumstances please" when the whole time, we should be praying, "Lord change my **C**haracter please." Understand, I am not saying that trials and distresses are in any way easy, believe me when I tell you I know what it is like to be in the valley, but God does not want us to bemoan our circumstances, He wants us to embrace it and understand this one truth, *These have come so that your faith – of greater worth than gold, which perishes even though refined by fire – may be proved genuine and may result in praise , glory and honor when Jesus Christ is revealed (1ˢᵗ Peter 1:7).* Any time I have ever read about great blessing in a believer's life or in the life of a local church fellowship, I have learnt one important thing, there was always a lowering first.

I love the story of the family who went away on holiday and they all shared the same room in a Bed & Breakfast. In the morning the little girl got into her mum and dad's bed, behind their bed was a picture of Jesus, in front of their bed was a huge mirror. The little girl began to rise up and then down and this continued until, after a few minutes she shouted, "Mummy, daddy, come quickly." When the parents came over the little girl said, "Look mummy and daddy, when I go up high I just see myself but when I lie low I just see Jesus." The lower we get the more we will see Christ, eliminating self can only lead to elevating Christ.

* THE LEVELLING – "Every mountain and hill shall be made low"

This is a very touchy one to mention with a lot of believers. You see, the hardest thing for any believer seems to be repentance, we talk about it all the time to those who are not saved but, when it comes to us and our lives as Christians, we seem to think that we are beyond it somehow. I think we would do well to get this right now, there has to be a lowering but equally there has to be a levelling. Can we get real here before God? All of us, writer included, need the levelling. Let me highlight for you five areas of our lives that we need to level out:

(i) **B**itterness – Oh this is the number one root cause of division within the church today, you know how petty we are in our fellowships sometimes. I have witnessed bitterness between sisters because one pavlova was one inch higher than the other. I have witnessed bitterness between brothers because one opened the window as they were too warm and the other one closed it because they were too cold and bitterness resulted, *See to it that no one misses the grace of God and that no bitter root grows up to cause trouble and defile many (Hebrews 12:15).*

(ii) **B**rokenness – Have you ever been here, when fellow believers have hurt you, slandered you and left you broken? I have been there you know, many believers come to church and it is like the panel on X-factor and when the preacher gets up to preach, it is as if he is standing on the red cross on the floor and waiting for some of the congregation to rate his performance and he is listening for the buzzer sound. Or maybe some of the congregation wait until they get home and when they get home and take out the electric knife to carve the Sunday roast they carve up some other believer or the preacher at the same time. All of this leaves people broken and brokenness is hard to heal. Can I tell you two verses that brought healing into my life? *Therefore, since we are surrounded by such a great cloud of witnesses, let us throw off everything that hinders and the sin that so easily entangles, and let us run with perseverance the race marked out for us. Let us fix our eyes on Jesus the author and perfecter of our faith, who for the joy set before him endured the cross, scorning its shame, and sat down at the right hand of the throne of God (Hebrews 12: 1- 2).*

(iii) **B**areness - This is maybe you, remember when the flame burned brightly for Him, you can recall outreach and telling others about the wonderful Saviour but, over the months and years, you have become disillusioned and barren and you need to cry from your heart, *wash away all my iniquity and cleanse me from my sin (Psalm 51:12).* Thank God there is healing for you, God promises in His word if you genuinely repent that He will restore you, *"I will repay you for the years that the locusts have eaten – the great locust and the young locust, the other locusts and the locust swarm – my great army that I sent among you. You will have plenty to eat, until you are full, and you will praise the name of the Lord your God, who has worked wonders for* *you; never again will my people be shamed. Then you will know that I am in Israel, that I am the Lord your God, and that there is no other; never again will my people be shamed" (Joel 2:25 - 27).*

(iv) **B**oldness – Many in church fellowships have this characteristic and it is not a nice one to have, you see they have failed to understand that the moment they professed to be saved there was a change ought to have happened, *Therefore, if anyone is in Christ, he is a new creation; the old has gone, the new has come (2ⁿᵈ Corinthians 5:17).* These people seem to have the attitude, 'I just say what I think' it does not matter how it hurts or what disruption it causes. Please understand, if you profess to be saved there ought to be a change, you are not your own anymore, you are bought with a price. So often, when I hear and observe what some believers say and do to others I just have to wonder if there has really been a life changing experience at all.

(v) **B**ashfulness - some people do not see bashfulness as a wrong that needs rectified but I want to make it clear that when it comes to speaking out and standing up for what we believe, bashfulness is a sin. This is how Mary looked upon this, *His mother said to the servants, "Do whatever he tells you" (John 2:5).* We are all guilty of this sin at times, there are many occasions when we should be and ought to be speaking out for our Saviour but yet we are timid and take on this bashful attitude that we cannot speak for Him. This is wrong and it needs to be levelled out.

- THE **L**INING – " The crooked shall be made straight"

Big problem this, I have come to note in my own personal life that my vision is not straight at times, in fact it is just simply crooked and I need to line up spiritually correctly in order for God to bless me. Often my focus was, and is, on so many other things, I want the Lord to bless this, I want the Lord to bless that. Yet the Word of God is also clear on another aspect of blessing, we are exhorted to bless the Lord, *"I will extol the Lord at all times; his praise will always be on my lips" (Psalm34:1)*. Many believers are so often looking for spiritual gifts and they come and say, "You know Marc I would just love It," but they are not lined up properly, their vision is all wrong, it is not about wanting it, **it is about wanting Him!!!** A.D Simpson wrote this and I never ever get tired of reading it,

> **Once it was the blessing,**
> **Now it is the Lord,**
> **Once it was the feeling,**
> **Now it is His word,**
> **Once His gift I wanted,**
> **Now the giver own,**
> **Once I sought for healing,**
> **Now Himself alone.**
> **All in all forever,**
> **Only Christ I'll sing,**
> **Everything is in Christ,**
> **And Christ in everything.**

Look again in Isaiah 57 vs.15 look at where the Lord dwells, *I dwell in the high and holy place.* Oh yes, we have to be brought low in order to look high, do you need your vision made straight? There is no better way to have your vision realigned than to have your mindset changed. Here is what Paul wrote to the Christians at Colosse, *Set your minds on things above, not on earthly things (Colossians 3:2).*

- THE LONGING – "The rough places made plain"

The bottom line is this, what you and I long for, that is what we will go after, *For where your treasure is, there your heart will be also (Matthew 6:21)*. We read it and we sing it sometimes, *As the deer pants for the streams of water, so my soul pants for you, O God. My soul thirsts for God, for the living God. When can I go and meet with God? (Psalm 42: 1-2)*. We all have priorities but, unless God is central in our lives then please do not be holding out for revival, you see you have got to Long for Him, Live for Him, Learn from Him, Look for Him. It's all about Him, *And he is the head of the body, the church; and he is the beginning and the firstborn from among the dead, so that in everything he might have the supremacy (Colossians 1:18)*.

A 12 year old boy became a Christian during a revival and the next week when he got back to school his friends started to question him about his experience, "Did you see a vision?" asked one. "Did you hear God speak asked another." The boy said, "No" to these questions and then they asked, "Well how do you know you are saved then?" The young boy thought for a moment and then said this, "It's like when you go to catch a fish, you can't see the fish, or hear the fish but you know you have it when you feel it tugging on the line." That is it, oh that He would tug on the line to our hearts right now and draw us closer to Himself.

Duncan Campbell said, "Revival is when a community of people are saturated by God."

I wanted the blessings and I still do but I was beginning to become fully aware of the conditions needed and required before God to experience and enjoy them. How deluded we Christians have become if we feel we can live how we like, go where we like, say what we like and then expect God to bless us. The Bible is clear on this, *If I had cherished sin in my heart, the Lord would not have listened (Psalm 66:18).*

I began to appreciate that one key area of any Christian's life had to be the time spent in the presence of God, in other words, prayer. It was not religion that God longed for but a relationship. I have learnt in my lifetime that relationships need to be worked at. If you and I want to get to know someone better then we have to spend time with them. So what is prayer? Prayer is the means whereby we can come into direct contact with the living God. To think that the God of the universe wants to, longs to have communion with me amazes me every single day. There is no long queuing process, I need not book an appointment, this access into the presence of God is immediate and it has been made possible through a new and living way, *by a new and living way opened for us through the curtain, that is, his body (Hebrews 10:20).* There are so many powerful prayers that I could refer to in the scriptures but I feel that there is no prayer more profound and one that really touches Heaven than the prayer of the Lord Jesus Christ in the Garden of Gethsemane.

There are two obstacles to passionate prayer, one is making time to pray and the other is weakness in the flesh. What I mean by weakness in the flesh could be explained under two things that we will easily be able to identify with:

1. Stress - This is anxiety that is ultimately fuelled by our lack of trust and dependence upon God and our own self-sufficiency.
2. Distress – The pressure that is placed upon us by the weight of a world that is ravished by sin.
   If I was to be desperate for God, if I was sincerely wanting Him to move in power in my life then I needed to spend time with Him, I loved to sing the words of William. D Longstaff's hymn:

1. Take time to be holy, speak oft with thy Lord;
Abide in Him always, and feed on His Word.
Make friends of God's children, help those who are weak,
Forgetting in nothing His blessing to seek.

2. Take time to be holy, the world rushes on;
Spend much time in secret, with Jesus alone.
By looking to Jesus, like Him thou shalt be;
Thy friends in thy conduct His likeness shall see.

3. Take time to be holy, let Him be thy Guide;
And run not before Him, whatever betide.
In joy or in sorrow, still follow the Lord,
And, looking to Jesus, still trust in His Word.

4. Take time to be holy, be calm in thy soul,
Each thought and each motive beneath His control.
Thus led by His Spirit to fountains of love,
Thou soon shalt be fitted for service above.

What was it then that Jesus prayed while in the Garden of Gethsemane? *Going a little farther, he fell with his face to the ground and prayed, "My Father, if it is possible, may this cup be taken from me. Yet not as I will, but as you will" (Matthew 26:39).* In this prayer there were four key things that seem to be the secret in touching the throne of God.

1. Evaluation - During this heartfelt cry to the Father, the Lord Jesus Christ opens up His heart. The Lord Jesus is bearing the innermost parts of His very soul and what He is asking the Father is this, "Is there any other way this plan of redemption can be accomplished? Is this the only means?" To pray effectively we ought to have the right evaluation of ourselves, yes God knows our hearts, but He wants to hear from our

hearts. The Psalmist said, *"Search me O God, and know my heart; test me and know my anxious thoughts. See if there is any offensive way in me, and lead me in the way everlasting" (Psalm 139:23-24).*

2. Elimination - *"Not as I will, but as you will."* How often do we pray and in our hearts we have already determined that we would like the Lord to answer it in the way that best suits us? I had to learn and yes I am still learning that it is not about what I want that matters it is about the will of God for my life that should be paramount.

3. Expectation – R.A. Torrey said, "The devil is not afraid of machinery, he is only afraid of God." When I pray do I expect God to answer? Do I even believe in the person to whom I am talking to? Oh that I would pray expecting God to answer, believing in whom I am talking to. So many times the answers that we receive are not the answers that we are expecting, but yet by faith we must understand fully that how God moves and how He answers is for our Eternal **G**ood and His Eternal **G**lory.

4. Endurance - Three times the Lord Jesus comes before God, He is not giving up, He understands that prayer takes endurance and in order to make intimate contact with the Father there has to be persistence. The Lord Jesus Christ spoke in a wonderful parable about this very matter, *Then he said to them, "Suppose one of you has a friend, and he goes to him at midnight and says, 'Friend, lend me three loaves of bread, because a friend of mine on a journey has come to me, and I have nothing to set before him.' "Then the one inside answers, 'Don't bother me. The door is already locked, and my children are with me in bed. I can't get up and give you anything.' I tell you, though he will not get up and give him bread because he is his friend, yet because of the man's boldness he will get up and give him as much as*

he needs. So I say to you: Ask and it will be given unto you; seek and you will find; knock and the door will be opened to you. For everyone who asks receives; he who seeks finds; and to him who knocks, the door will be opened. "Which of you fathers, if your son asks for a fish, will give him a snake instead? Or if he asks for an egg, will give him a scorpion? If you then, though you are evil, know how to give good gifts to your children, how much more will your Father in heaven give the Holy Spirit to those who ask him!" (Luke 11: 5-13).

The blessings could only come when a true relationship was established with the Father. I was willing to ask, seek and knock. God is not some distant, harsh emotionally detached person that is constantly standing with a huge cane ready to punish us. God, wants to have fellowship with us, it is His heart's desire to lavish blessing upon His children, but we must come to Him with the right approach and in the right attitude. On a very practical note, I find in my own Christian walk that in keeping a prayer diary or a pray list if there is something that you feel needs prayer, then write it down. Pray until it is answered and then with joy, (whether the answer is what you want or not) mark that request from the list.

God, Your grace, mercy and blessings are far beyond my human understanding. The very fact that the God of all Glory loves me overwhelms my soul with deep gratitude and joy. I know that there must be and ought to be a clear view on who I am and who God really is, and there are so many fleshy pieces still left around this heart of mine. There has to be refining, there must be an open exposure to all areas of my life, after all You alone know me intimately because You formed me and knew me in my mother's womb. Search me Oh God, know my heart I pray, see if there be some wicked way in me, cleanse me from every stain and set me free. In Jesus name, Amen.

CHAPTER SIX

BLINDED

Ephesians 1:18 I pray also that the eyes of your heart may be enlightened in order that you may know the hope to which he has called you, the riches of his glorious inheritance in the saints

This was exciting, the Holy Spirit was doing a work in my heart but what was going on? I was hearing so many different expressions being hurtled about - "Baptism of the Spirit," "Anointing of the Spirit," "The Second Blessing" and "Slain in the Spirit." This all sounded so good and all very well but even the Christians I knew who used these expressions could not agree what the correct phraseology was. I loved what Billy Graham said, "I don't care what you call it, just make sure you get it" and that sounded like wise council to me. I was humble enough and sincere enough to understand this, the moment that I became a child of God, right at that very moment something supernatural and wonderful took place, the Holy Spirit entered and took up residence within me and I was indwelt by the Holy Spirit and sealed by the Spirit of the living God. When I delved into the Bible I discovered something deeper and very real, in the Old Testament it was apparent that the Spirit came upon people and equipped them for certain tasks and ministries but the Spirit could leave them again. In the New Testament however, the Spirit was not just to come upon a believer, He was to dwell in the believer and furthermore the Spirit could be experienced in all His fullness for different tasks and ministries when, as believers we are willing to yield ourselves fully to Him. The Holy Spirit, once indwelling a believer, was now not going to leave them because the assurance is given in the Bible when it says, *And you also were included in Christ when you heard the word of truth, the gospel of your salvation. Having believed, you were marked in him with a seal, the promised Holy Spirit, who is a deposit guaranteeing our inheritance until the redemption of those who are God's possession – to the praise of his glory (Ephesians 1: 13-14).* But yet, as I continued reading the Word of God and asking the Spirit to lead me into all truth, there were many things that started to be graciously and wonderfully revealed to me. Questions fluttered through my mind. What made Peter afraid to tell people in the courtyard that he knew Jesus? What was it then that gave him the strength to speak in front of thousands? What did Paul mean when he said to the believers in Ephesus, *Do not get drunk on wine, which leads to debauchery. Instead, be filled with the Spirit (Ephesians 5:18).* If the indwelling of the Holy Spirit was the only solitary teaching of the New Testament to the believers why then is there so much mentioned about the fullness of the Holy Spirit? It was evident to me that to every single believer there was a bigger teaching to be found in relation to the work of the Holy Spirit. I had been blinded to this amazing truth, there was more!!! It was not that I was to receive more of the Holy Spirit, the fact was that the Holy Spirit had to receive more of me.

So the searching continued. Now please understand, this was not something that had to be worked up or something that God had available to a select few, not at all, but what I was fully aware of was this, the fullness of the Holy Spirit would not be demonstrated in all His fullness in the life of someone who had never understood the fact and biblical truth that they are dead but spiritually alive in Christ. How precious it was when for that first time the Holy Spirit revealed the sacred truth to me as I read, *I have been crucified with Christ and I no longer live, but Christ lives in me. The life that I live in the body, I live by faith in the Son of God, who loved me and gave himself for me (Galatians 2:20).* I had sung heartily so many times the words of Sally Ellis,

It's no longer I that liveth,
But Christ that liveth in me.
It's no longer I that liveth,
But Christ that liveth in me.
He lives, He lives,
Jesus is alive in me!
It's no longer I that liveth,
But Christ that liveth in me.

But yet I knew that these were no more than empty words to me, of course it was me still living, I had to understand that I needed to die.

Let me explain in a very simple way. Drugs are prevalent in every community, town, city and country. Presently in Northern Ireland there is a huge advertising campaign ongoing issued by the Police Service Of Northern Ireland. The intention of course is to deal with the scourge of drugs in our society, however this is only dealing with the problem locally and by no means is it erasing the problem completely of drug abuse. Why? In order for illegal drugs to be eradicated we have to get to the root problem, the drug barons and the secret factories that produce and manufacture the substances, it is there that the drug problem can be dealt with in totality. So it is with this teaching in this verse, it is the blood that cleanses and deals with the product produced i.e. my sin, but it is the cross that deals with the factory that produces the sin i.e. the old man, he has to be crucified. Some dear Christians have distorted this truth and not only have they crucified the old man which is what they are supposed to do, but they have crucified the new man too and their very countenance makes them void of displaying Christ in all His beauty and glory. *You were taught, with regard to your former way of life, to put off your old self, which is being corrupted by its deceitful desires; to be made new in the attitude of your minds (Ephesians 4 vs.22-23).* It is the **"putting off, in order to put on."**

What a revelation, to understand that I am dead and Christ lives in me and for me and through me. The blindness that I had believed to be the norm was lifted, 'the more' that Christ wanted for His children I was beginning to understand and the fullness of the Holy Spirit was beginning to become meaningful to me as clearly taught in New Testament scripture.

It would do us no harm at all to have another Selah at this point and look at the scripture again as to the teaching and the work of The Holy Spirit.

DEUTERONOMY 31 VS.9-13 JOHN 7 VS.37-39 & ACTS 19 VS.1-7 & EPHESIANS 5 VS.18

This is a massive subject and one that so many Bible believing evangelical Christians for some reason, are afraid of. Of course as I have previously mentioned we believe in the Father, the Son and the Holy Spirit and we hold the doctrine of the Triune God very dearly and we preach about God and who He is and we speak about the Lord Jesus Christ but when it comes to the Holy Spirit we seem a little bit apprehensive to go there. Now there are reasons for this I know because many people have taken the Holy Spirit to lengths that go beyond the boundary of scripture so therefore any mention of Him at all and we tend to shut up shop. I want us to understand that the Holy Spirit is the key to Conviction, to Conversion and to Continuation.

If ever there was a day when we need revival in the Holy Spirit then it is today. We pray in the meetings so often that the Holy Spirit will convict men, women and young people about their need of a Saviour but yet when it comes to the work of the Holy Spirit after salvation we seem to be so afraid. If the early church Christians were back amongst us in our churches today they would get the shock of their lives. They did not have a building because the first public building for the church was not ready for about 300 years after the book of Acts was written, they did not have PowerPoint or a classy sound system or strophe lighting or anything like this but what they did have what most of our churches do not have is the dynamic power of the Holy Spirit. In case any believers feel that I am speaking out of turn and you feel that anything in relation to the Holy Spirit is received at the moment of conversion and that is the end of things, the Word of God disagrees with such a viewpoint, *Now to each one the manifestation of the Spirit is given for the common good. To one there is given through the Spirit the message of wisdom, to another the message of knowledge by means of the same Spirit, to another the gifts of healing by that one Spirit, to another miraculous powers, to another prophecy, to another distinguishing between spirits, to another speaking in different kinds of tongues and still to another the interpretation of tongues, all these are the work of the one and same Spirit, and he gives them to each one, just as he determines (1st Corinthians 12:7 - 11).* The important thing to notice in these verses that three times Paul underlines that all of these gifts come from the "one Spirit". The Word of God makes a special ruling on anything that is threefold, *Though one may be overpowered, two can defend themselves. A cord of three strands is not quickly broken (Ecclesiastes 4:12).* To abolish the gifts of the Holy Spirit is to discredit the Word of God.

What I want to do is simply echo the cry of Isaiah the prophet when he cried, *Oh, that you would rend the heavens and come down, that the mountains would tremble before you! As when fire sets twigs ablaze and causes water to boil, come down to make your name known to your enemies and cause the nations to quake before you! For when you did awesome things that we did not expect you came down, and the mountains trembled before you (Isaiah 64 vs.1-3).*

The readings that I have suggested begin in Deuteronomy 31, followed by John 7. Again I suggest that we look at these passages in the King James Version to receive the explanation. Before we commence, we need to get the picture in our minds of the backdrop to what the Lord Jesus is teaching in relation to the Holy Spirit. Tabernacles were a popular festival, rich in symbolism. Each day of the Feast of Tabernacles included a water ceremony in which a procession of priests descended to the southern border of the city to the Gihon Spring (which flowed into the Pool of Siloam). There a priest filled a golden pitcher as a choir chanted Isaiah 12:3: *"With joy you will draw water from the wells of salvation."* The water was then carried back up the hill to the "Water Gate," followed by crowds carrying tree branches (lulab in the right hand) in memory of the desert booths and (an ethrog in the left hand) a citrus branch in memory of the harvest. The crowd would shake these and sing in full voice Psalms 113–118. When the procession arrived at the temple, the priest would climb the altar steps and pour the water onto the altar while the crowd circled him and continued singing. On the seventh day of the festival, this procession took place seven times. In this very ceremony we can see what religion requires, religion promises ritual with no reality, whereas Christ is going to promise reality without religion.

Judaism saw this water ceremony on several levels. On the one hand, it was a plea to God for rain since the autumn is a time of threatened drought in Israel. On the other hand, it was a source of rich symbolism. The feast was established as a memorial to the wilderness journey and God's provision of water from a rock (Numbers. 20:8, 10). The pouring out of water which caused the sacrificial rock altar of the temple to flow represented the day God's life giving water would flow out of God's temple during the Messianic age. Zechariah and Ezekiel had visions of rivers flowing from the temple in a miraculous display of God's blessing that they record for us in (Ezekiel. 47:1 & Zechariah. 14:8). In a drought-stricken land, it was a spectacular vision of water, life-giving water flowing from God's life-giving temple.

Now, with this backdrop in mind, I want to look at the three New Testament readings that I have recommended you read and point out five amazing, practical things for us to learn.

- ## THE CRY –

On this final day of celebration, Jesus steps into public view and makes His most stunning pronouncement of the feast. As the seventh water procession climbed the steep hill of south Jerusalem, verse 37 commences, *In the last day, that great day of the feast, Jesus stood and cried, saying, If any man thirst, let him come unto me, and drink.*

In John 7 we read about a planned and prepared appearance of Jesus Christ on the final day of the symbolic Jewish festival. He stood up in their midst as someone who was an uninvited preacher and cried out. The word **'cried'** means **'shouted loudly and emphatically'** so that all might hear and heed. Surely, we all would agree that most believers are thirsty for the Holy Spirit. But yet, we are trying everything and anything else to get this thirst quenched and we are the ones crying out for something more in our Christian lives and yet the cry comes from Christ, "if you are thirsty come to Me and drink." We wonder why we spend so much time living in Romans chapter 6 & 7, it is because we are not thirsting after the only thing that can quench the thirst and that is Christ.

In order to have the Holy Spirit in all of His fullness we need to get back to the very essence and basics of the Christian faith, so often we only preach a half gospel but when you hear the full gospel it transforms lives and really changes people. "What do you mean?" someone may ask. You see the more I live in my Christian life I understand that reconciliation and salvation are two separate things but two things that are a must and a necessity for every believer. What do I mean, again you might ask? Let me refer you to the clarity of scripture, *For if, when we were God's enemies, we were reconciled to him through the death of his Son, how much more, having been reconciled, shall we be saved through his life! (Romans 5:10).* You see this is the full gospel, not just a half gospel, He reconciles you to God by His death, but He saves you on a daily basis because of His risen life. So often so many evangelists, pastors and teachers leave Christ on the cross. I am fully aware of the basic fundamental truth that we need the blood of Christ that was shed upon the cross, *In fact, the law requires that nearly everything be cleansed with blood, and without the shedding of blood there is no forgiveness (Hebrews 9:22).* But to leave Christ on the cross brings a terrible injustice upon the work of redemption, Christ is no longer on the cross or is He in the grave. Jesus Christ is alive and the power that we can experience for victorious Christian living is in His risen life. Let those of us that have this Heavenly responsibility of preaching, do so in resurrection power.

Allow me to share one of my favourite verses, *The mystery that has been kept hidden for ages and generations, but is now disclosed to the saints. To them God has chosen to make known among the Gentiles the glorious riches of this mystery, which is Christ in you, the hope of glory (Colossians 1:26 -27).*

Can you see the difference? Major W. Ian Thomas in his book The Saving Life of Christ (Pg20) said:

To be in Christ that is redemption, but for Christ to be in you that is sanctification.

To be in Christ that makes you fit for heaven, but for Christ to be in you that makes you fit for earth

To be in Christ that changes your destination, but for Christ to be in you that changes your destiny.

What I love about Paul is this, **Paul did not see the resurrection of Jesus Christ as One Man's victory but he saw it as victory for all men. Jesus did not just get a new life, He gave new life.**

- ## THE CONDITION –

He that believeth on me, as the scripture hath said, out of his belly shall flow rivers of living water (John 7:38). Now in order for you and me to have the fullness of the Spirit we must drink. There are countless scriptures to show us that the Holy Spirit is spoken of in relation to drinking of course one of the Bible favourites is this one, *Come, all you who are thirsty, come to the waters, and you who have no money, come, buy and eat! Come, buy wine and milk without money and without cost (Isaiah 55:1).* I want us to grasp the importance of this the fact, that when we drink deeply from Christ not only will it bring a refreshing and a fullness of the Spirit to you personally but it will also outpour into the lives of others. I am not sure if any of you have ever been to the Dead Sea, it is called the Dead Sea for a very apparent and interesting reason. There are no fish or plant life in it because of the content of salt and the reason behind this is that the Dead Sea has got an inlet which flows in from Jordan but it has no outlets, so you get the idea, inlets plus no outlets equals Dead Sea. Now let me apply this spiritually. If we read, download messages, study the Word of God and constantly feel we have to take in and then discover that we are not fruitful in our Christian lives it is because we have so many inlets and no outlets that we become dead Christians, just like the Dead Sea.

- ## THE COMMENCEMENT –

In the Old Testament time and time again you will read that the Spirit of the Lord came upon people for very specific tasks, *Then the Spirit of the Lord came upon Gideon, and he blew a trumpet, summoning the Abiezrites to follow him (Judges 6:34). Then the Spirit of the Lord came upon Jephthah. He crossed Gilead and Manasseh, passed through Mizpah of Gilead, and from there he advanced against the Ammonites (Judges 11:29). So Samuel took the horn of oil and anointed him in the presence of his brothers, and from that day on the Spirit of the Lord came upon David in power. Samuel then went to Ramah (1ˢᵗ Samuel 16:13).* But when the Spirit of The Lord came upon individuals it also could leave individuals, *Now the Spirit of the Lord had departed from Saul, and an evil Spirit from the Lord tormented him (1ˢᵗ Samuel 16:14). Then she called, "Samson, the Philistines are upon you!" he awoke from his sleep and thought, "I'll go out as before and shake myself free." But he did not know that the Lord had left him (Judges 16:20).* But in the New Testament something different was going to happen as we have already mentioned earlier, the Holy Spirit was not just going to come upon people for special tasks and then leave them, the Holy Spirit was going to come like never before and indwell believers and not leave them. *I baptize you with water, but he will baptize you with the Holy Spirit (Mark 1:8).*

John answered them all, "I baptize you with water, but one more powerful than I will come, the thongs of whose sandals I am not worthy to untie. He will baptize you with the Holy Spirit and with fire (Luke 3:16). So when was this going to commence? *(But this spake he of the Spirit, which they that believe on him should receive: for the Holy Ghost was not yet given; because that Jesus was not yet glorified.) (John 7:39).* We must understand what John is implying here by saying this, he is intentionally linking the Lord Jesus Christ and the Holy Spirit in order to give us the precise understanding of the origin of the Holy Spirit and his relationship to the Lord Jesus Christ. The fullness, baptism or gift of the Spirit whatever you would like to call this, was not available while Jesus was engaged in His earthly ministry. There had to be the glorification, that means Jesus had to die, be buried, and be raised again the third day according to the scriptures and then be exalted and seated at the right hand of the Father in order for the 'Comforter' to come. So you get the order here because it is a Divine order, Calvary must come before the Resurrection and the Ascension must come before Pentecost, it was a glorified Saviour that released the Holy Spirit, the Comforter. The word used is **"parakletos',"** pronounced **"par-ak'-lay-tos"** meaning, **"an intercessor, consoler:--advocate, comforter."** He came to finish the work that God began in Christ but He could not begin His work until Christ had accomplished His work. We have already mentioned this amazing verse, *And afterward, I will pour out my Spirit on all people. Your sons and daughters will prophesy, your old men will dream dreams, your young men will see visions: (Joel 2:28).* So when did this commence and has this concluded? We all know that the commencement of the Holy Spirit's work in a new way like never before happened on the day of Pentecost in Acts 2 but the coming of the Holy Spirit was going to be unforgettable, nothing like this was seen before as He now comes with visible and unforgettable evidences of wind and fire. Wind is a sign of God's Spirit as both the Greek and Hebrew words for Spirit indicate. Fire was also a symbol of the divine presence as seen in the numerous Old Testament events such as the burning bush (Exodus. 3:2-5), the pillar of cloud by day and fire by night that guided the Israelites in their wilderness journey (Exodus. 13:21), the consuming fire on Mt. Sinai (Exodus. 24:17) and the pillar of fire that rested over the tabernacle in the desert (Exodus. 40:38). God once again is present among His people in a mighty way. So how and what way did the Holy Spirit commence and what can I personally learn about the coming of the Holy Spirit at Pentecost?

- The Power of the Holy Spirit – *You are witnesses of these things, I am going to send you what my father has promised; but stay in the city until you have been clothed with power from on high. (Luke 24: 48-49).*

- The Place of the Holy Spirit - *Don't you know that you yourselves are God's temple and that God's Spirit lives in you? (1st Corinthians. 3:16).*

- The Potential of the Holy Spirit - *Do not get drunk on wine, which leads to debauchery. Instead, be filled with the Spirit (Ephesians. 5:18).*

- The Purpose of the Holy Spirit - *As for you, the anointing you received from him remains in you, and you do not need anyone to teach you. But as his anointing teaches you about all things and as just as that anointing is real, not counterfeit – just as it has taught you, remain in him (1ˢᵗ John 2:27).*

- The Presence of the Holy Spirit - *But I tell you the truth: it is for your good that I am going away. Unless I go away, the Counsellor will not come to you (John 16:7).*

- THE CONFUSION –

So why then is there so much confusion surrounding the Holy Spirit? Well a great deal of confusion comes from the passage in Acts 19. We have got to understand Paul, at Ephesus, found some religious people who looked to Jesus as the Messiah. They had not been led to expect the miraculous powers of the Holy Ghost nor were they informed that the gospel was especially the ministration of the Spirit. Paul shows them that John never designed that those he baptized should rest there, but told them that they should believe on him who should come after him, that is, on the Lord Jesus Christ. They thankfully accepted the discovery and were baptized in the name of the Lord Jesus. The Holy Ghost came upon them in a surprising, overpowering manner, they spoke with tongues, and prophesied, as the apostles and the first Gentile converts did. Now I am well aware that some people might look at verse 1 and say that these people here were called 'disciples' but wait, just because the term 'disciple' is used here does not automatically mean that these disciples were saved, if you recall the scriptures tells us that *"many of Jesus disciples followed Him no more" (John 6:66).* The very fact that they were relying on the baptism of John and not the work of Christ would suggest to me that they were seeking, but as yet, had not found the truth. That aside let me scripturally show you what happens at salvation in relation to the Holy Spirit and what happens subsequently.

AT SALVATION

- Born of the Spirit – *Jesus answered, "I tell you the truth, no one can enter the kingdom of God unless he is born of water and the Spirit" (John 3:5).*

- Baptised by the Spirit - *For all of you who were baptized into Christ have clothed yourselves with Christ (Galatians 3:27).*

- Bodily Indwelt by the Spirit – *Do you not know that your body is a temple of the Holy Spirit, who is in you, whom you have received from God? You are not your own; you were bought at a price. Therefore honor God with your body (1st Corinthians 6:19-20).*

- Blessedly Sealed by the Spirit - *And do not grieve the Holy Spirit of God, with whom you were sealed for that day of redemption (Ephesians 4:30).*

AFTER SALVATION

- Filled by the Spirit - - *Do not get drunk on wine, which leads to debauchery. Instead, be filled with the Spirit (Ephesians 5:18).* The word "**filled**" is the word "**pleroo**," pronounced "**play-ro'-o**" this means "**to make replete, i.e. (literally) to cram (a net), level up (a hollow), or (figuratively) to furnish (or imbue, diffuse, influence), satisfy, execute (an office), finish (a period or task), verify (or coincide with a prediction), etc.:--accomplish, X after, (be) complete, end, expire, fill (up), fulfil, (be, make) full (come), fully preach, perfect, supply.**"

- Faithful to the Spirit - What I mean by this, is that when you rely on the leading and guiding of the Holy Spirit and let Him control you, then for every special task the Holy Spirit will anoint you with a special touch to deal with that task, if we remain faithful.

- THE CONTINUATION –

  Now we only scratched the surface in respect to the Holy Spirit so let me just finish with the continuation of the work of the Holy Spirit: *And afterward, I will pour out my Spirit on all people. Your sons and daughters will prophesy, your old men will dream dreams, your young men will see visions: (Joel 2:28).* Now that we have observed how the gifts and manifestations of the Holy Spirit commenced, the big question is, why do some people believe that this has stopped? Of course they will take you automatically to the verse I referred to earlier, *But when perfection comes, the imperfect disappears (1 Corinthians 13:10).* So let us gain some insight into this verse because it is misinterpreted in so many different evangelical circles, here is the correct rendering of the words **'is come'** it carries with it the following meaning, **'does come; or shall come'.** This proposition is couched in a general form. This means that when anything which is perfect is seen or enjoyed, then that which is imperfect is forgotten, laid aside, or vanishes. So in the full and perfect light of a sunny day when the sun is shining with not a cloud of hindrance, the imperfect and feeble light of the stars and moon although however bright, vanishes they are soon forgotten. The sense here is that in Heaven, and only in Heaven, where there is a state of absolute perfection, that which is 'in part,' or which is imperfect, shall be lost in light of Heaven's superior brightness. All imperfection will vanish. All that we now possess that is obscure and imperfect in this old world that is rotten with sin shall be lost in the superior and perfect glory of that eternal world. All our present unsatisfactory modes of obtaining knowledge shall be unknown, no matter how we try to attain to personal perfection (and we ought to be following in Christ's steps as Christians) we will never be perfect while in this world. All shall be clear, bright, and eternal one day. It is only in the eternal state when sin, Satan and this world will be dealt with in totality that all things will be made perfect so until then let us not be 'pick n mix' Christians, let us take the Word of God as what it says and apply it to our lives, let me please reiterate this passage once more, *There are different kinds of gifts, but the same Spirit. There are different kinds of service, but the same Lord. There are different kinds of working, but the same God works all of them in all men. Now to each one the manifestation of the Spirit is given for the common good. To one there is given through the Spirit the message of wisdom, to another the message of knowledge by means of the same Spirit, to another the gifts of healing by that one Spirit, to another miraculous powers, to another prophecy, to another distinguishing between spirits, to another speaking in different kinds of tongues and still to another the interpretation of tongues, all these are the work of the one and same Spirit, and he gives them to each one, just as he determines (1Corinthians 12:4 -11).*

I know so many believers who would just love all the gifts of the Holy Spirit, but Paul exhorts us ,*But eagerly desire the greater gifts (1ˢᵗ Corinthians 12:31).*Paul then continues to write and takes a great deal of time in teaching in chapter thirteen of 1ˢᵗ Corinthians about love. He concludes my writing, *And now these three remain: faith, hope and love. But the greatest of these is love (1ˢᵗ Corinthians 13:13).*

I am humble enough and honest enough before God to understand that the manifestation and the work and the gifts of the Holy Spirit are still here today. I love this quote:

You have to stay a little closer
You have to go a little farther
You have to want a little better

When the Holy Spirit comes on a believer,
He makes Christ dearer
Heaven a whole lot nearer
The Word of God a lot clearer.

It may well be that you are still somewhat confused by this massive subject of the fullness of the Spirit and it could be that the question on your lips is, "How do I move on into the good of this experience in my Christian life?" So often in my own Christian experience I have tried to create a 'good feeling' or tried to work up some wonderful spiritual experience, even at times when I have been engaged in preaching I have tried so desperately hard to make it a 'good sermon' with loads of passion, emotion and energy. The reality is, the spiritual cannot be 'worked up' this is a Divine encounter with a Divine God.

Frances Ridley Havergal on the night of February 4th, 1874, penned one of her most well known and well loved hymns. This hymn was written as a result of a Divine Encounter that took place at Areley House. Frances had gone for a five day visit and while she was there ten other people were present in the house also. Some of these people were Christians but others were not and so Frances prayed a simple but effective prayer, "Lord, give me all in this house!" Did God answer? Before Frances left the house every single person had a Divine Encounter with God, Frances explains, "I was too happy to sleep and so I passed the most of the night in praise and renewal of my own consecration and these little couplets formed themselves and chimed in my heart one after another till they finished with, 'Ever **ONLY, All** for Thee'. The lyrics of this hymn speak profoundly into my own life every time I sing them, the lyrics penetrate every area of our lives, from our Words to our Wallets, but yet the stark reality is that they can so often become repetitive words without having an impact on the very area that is meant to be addressed, Consecration.

Take my life, and let it be
Consecrated, Lord, to Thee;
Take my moments and my days,
Let them flow in ceaseless praise,
Let them flow in ceaseless praise.

Take my hands, and let them move
At the impulse of Thy love;
Take my feet and let them be
Swift and beautiful for Thee,
Swift and beautiful for Thee.

Take my voice, and let me sing
Always, only, for my King;
Take my lips, and let them be
Filled with messages from Thee,
Filled with messages from Thee.

Take my silver and my gold;
Not a mite would I withhold;
Take my intellect, and use
Every power as Thou shalt choose,
Every power as Thou shalt choose.

Take my will, and make it Thine;
It shall be no longer mine.
Take my heart; it is Thine own;
It shall be Thy royal throne,
It shall be Thy royal throne.

Take my love; my Lord, I pour
At Thy feet its treasure-store.
Take myself, and I will be
Ever, only, all for Thee,
Ever, only, all for Thee.

God wants His children not to be blinded, He longs for us to come into the blessings that are available to us through His resurrected life, but there are conditions that must be attained to in order for the Holy Spirit to perform a supernatural work within us. There is what I like to envisage as a 'Four Step Road' to experiencing the blessing of God.

1. Confession – Scripture suggests that there are several things that hold back the blessing of God. I have alluded to some earlier in the book but there are three key areas that we must address.

   • Sinfulness - *If I had cherished sin in my heart, the Lord would not have listened (Psalm 66:18).*

   • Stubbornness - *But they refused to pay attention; stubbornly they turned their backs and stopped their ears. They made their hearts as hard as flint and would not listen to the law or to the words that the Lord Almighty had sent by his Spirit through the earlier prophets. So the Lord Almighty was very angry (Zechariah 7:11-12).*

   • Selfishness – *You want something but don't get it. You kill and covet, but you cannot have what you want. You quarrel and fight. You do not have, because you do not ask God. When you ask, you do not receive, because you ask with wrong motives, that you may spend what you get on your own pleasures (James 4:2-3).*

When we deal with these matters it is then that 'our part' of the conditions are fulfilled. God is only willing to cover with His blood what we are willing to uncover. Be aware that I am not taking on a 'holier than thou' attitude, the reality of the three pronged attack of, world, flesh and the devil have stared me in the face even in the midst of writing this book. I am a man that is striving daily for more of God.

2. Cleansing - *But if we walk in the light, as he is in the light, we have fellowship with one another, and the blood of Jesus, his Son purifies us from all sin. If we claim to be without sin, we deceive ourselves and the truth is not in us. If we confess our sins, he is faithful and just and will forgive our sins and purify us from all unrighteousness (1ˢᵗ John 1: 7-9).*

3. Consecration – Two words that sometimes float so easily from our mouths without understanding the true significance and meaning are justification and sanctification. When we became Christians, in spite of the fact that we had sinned, God forgave us. But it is not that we are just forgiven, the truth and essence of this is that, God treats us just as if we had never sinned. *Therefore, since we have been justified through faith, we have peace with God through our Lord Jesus Christ (Romans 5:1).* When the "accuser of the brethren" comes with those attacks to rob us of joy and rake up past sins, God the judge observes that Jesus has paid the price for our sins and so acquits us and throws out those accusations from the devil and declares us, "Not Guilty." At this point sanctification begins. The work of sanctification is a process that is continual whereby the Holy Spirit brings us into a relationship with God in a fuller and deeper way. *To be a minister of Christ Jesus to the Gentiles with the priestly duty of proclaiming the gospel of God, so that the Gentiles might become an offering acceptable to God, sanctified by the Holy Spirit (Romans 15:16).*

4. Christlike - *For those God foreknew he also predestined to be conformed to the likeness of his Son, that he might be the firstborn among many brothers (Romans 15:29).* Paul in his writings to the Galatians gives clear guidance on someone who is Christlike in Character. *But the fruit of the Spirit is love, joy, peace, patience, kindness, goodness, faithfulness, gentleness and self-control (Galatians 5:22-23).*

It is striking to take note that this is one "fruit" but nine segments. I search my own heart as I also ask you, what fruit am I displaying?

Lord God we praise You for the work of the Holy Spirit, it was evident in our lives in conviction, it was the Holy Spirit that brought about our conversion, but God how we long for the blessed Holy Spirit to continue to work in our lives and our hearts. We praise You that we have not been left alone on this journey, and there is One who is there to draw alongside. Blessed Holy Spirit come we pray, lead us, guide us, work in us. In Jesus name, Amen.

CHAPTER SEVEN

BURDENED

John 4:35 Do you not say, 'Four months more and then harvest'? I tell you, open your eyes and look at the fields! They are ripe for harvest.

When one yields and summits to the Holy Spirit, it is not long before everything comes to you with what I like to refer to as 'Kingdom glasses' on. To see yourself the way Christ sees you, to see the world the way Christ sees it and to understand in some small part the compassion of the Saviour. One of the basic characteristics that should be manifested in every true believers heart is that of being passionate for souls. Right throughout the earthly ministry of our Lord Jesus Christ He was passionate about souls. How often do we read of Him taking time to tend to the needs of His fellow man? Of course the Pharisees could not understand this, *But the Pharisees and the teachers of the law muttered, "This man welcomes sinners and eats with them" (Luke15:2).* Thank God that Jesus received sinners because if He did not then that would rule every single one of us out from having a relationship with Him because the scripture says, *for all have sinned and fall short of the glory of God (Romans 3:23).*

I became so heavily burdened for my family and my friends there were so many years wasted and I was longing to make up for lost time for the Master. I knew the plan of the Lord Jesus Christ and the promise that His word gave was clear, *I will repay you for the years the locusts have eaten – the great locust and the young locust, the other locusts and the locust swarm – my great army that I sent among you (Joel 2:25).* I wanted to win souls to Christ, it was my heart's desire, I wanted it more than anything, just to be able to point even one to the beauty and the finished work of Calvary where the Lord Jesus Christ had shed His precious life giving blood to atone for their sins and to tell just one of the life that Christ wanted to live for them, when they received Him this is the very reason of why He said, "*The thief comes only to steal and kill and destroy; I have come that they may have life, and have it to the full*" *(John10:10).*

I turned to the book of Acts chapter 9 and I asked the question like Saul did, "Lord, what do you want me to do? In a clear leading of the Holy Spirit I was led immediately to this passage, *Andrew, Simon Peter's brother, was one of the two who had followed Jesus. The first thing Andrew did was to find his brother Simon and tell him, "We have found the Messiah" (that is, the Christ) (John 1:40-41).* I knew what this meant, of course in this context it was Andrew who was finding his brother but my brother was called Andrew and I was to find him.

Wonderful how the self centred man is never too far away. I had immediately thought that I was to get a hall somewhere in my home town and start youth meetings, I was putting plans into full swing but hold on a minute is that what God wants? Clearly it was not. Wait, God is the one who does the leading my role is to follow. God burdened me with a small hall in Stewartstown owned by the believers in Coagh Baptist Church. Believe me when I say I got a little bit of the Moses Syndrome when this was revealed to me, Why Stewartstown? Why me? What is there? So it was at the leading and guiding of the Holy spirit that I met with Mr W.G Orr one of the elders in Coagh Baptist Church, I could scarcely believe his reaction, the hall had been owned by these believers for some time and they had been praying for years for an effective witness in reaching out with the Gospel to be established there. I travelled home in my car and as I travelled these words echoed in my ear, *As for God, his way is perfect; the word of the Lord is flawless. He is a shield for all who take refuge in him (Psalm 18:30).*

Mr W.G Orr brought it to the members of the fellowship and it was agreed that the hall be given for the commencement of a Thursday night Bible study, prayer group and a youth meeting once a month to be convened on a Saturday night.

First night of bible study and prayer time, it was life changing. I turned up in Stewartstown at the little hall that hugs the side of the main road, switched on the heating and lighting and sat waiting for the folk to come. Almost half past eight and to my surprise no one came, so my first words, "Told you Lord this wasn't right." How I was rebuked, within a few weeks the Bible study and prayer meeting were growing rapidly with young people and not so young people coming before the Lord, broken and burdened just like me for their families. With humbleness of heart I confessed what I already knew to be right, "Lord, You are right, it is me who is wrong." How these prayer times were special, tears flowed and the presence of Christ was almost tangible.

I could not wait to see what God was going to do on our first Saturday night youth meeting. We met for prayer before it, and as we opened the door that led into the main hall we could do nothing only say, "Thank you God, thank you so much." The hall was packed to over flowing, and there in the very back seat was my brother, Andrew and all of his friends.

Masturbation, pornography, sexual experiences and homosexuality all things that became evident that these young people were struggling with, yet the churches were afraid to speak on these subjects thus leaving these young people carrying guilt and shame and the enemy rendering them powerless to do anything for the Lord Jesus. I knew how these young people felt I had been there myself, I had felt the pain, the isolation and the shame but yet I also understood the fact that there was victory in the Lord Jesus Christ. He had overcome Satan and He had conquered and in Him there could be found freedom from every struggle and every chain that binds.

How these nights were special and how they opened my eyes and understanding to the struggles and difficulties and temptations that so many young people were experiencing. On our very first night it was as if floodgates had opened we had so many young people that stayed behind for counselling, it seemed that the build up of many years were they could tell no one in their churches and not even their pastors for fear of shame and guilt and the thought that they would be isolated and left out to dry had suddenly been removed. Over the next few months an intense course of deliverance, genuine repentance and restoration to fellowship took place with Christ, today so many of these young people are serving the Lord effectively where God has placed them.

Church leaders, we need to sit up and take notice of the enemy and how he is seeking to rob young people of their usefulness in the work of Christ. We need to teach them about the saving life of Christ, who they are in Christ. The longer I serve the Lord the more apparent it becomes to me that all too often so many Christians are living in some 'fantasy Christian world' that teaches sinless perfection and claims that the enemy cannot have a hold on a believer's life. Shame on us!!

The Holy Spirit came in mighty power and moved in many hearts, lives were changed, young people were challenged, and to top it off although it was not my brother who came to the Lord at this stage, it was many of his friends, Praise God!! What a thrill that today The Rescue is still a centre in Stewartstown where young people meet to pray and the Saturday Night monthly meeting is still held. The most joyous thing to observe is that many who came to Christ as Saviour in the early years are now the leaders carrying on the work.

One of the highlights of this time at The Rescue was a Tent Crusade held in the field behind where we held The Rescue meetings. Mr. Stephen Law, my uncle Pastor John Taylor and myself were the speakers with different testimonies and singers nightly. God opened the windows of Heaven and poured out blessing and many people made a commitment to follow Christ.

It was during this amazing period of blessing that God began to stir up my nest, I was burdened intensely for souls and it was Uganda that seemed to be increasingly coming more and more before me, was God going to take our little family there? I recalled so vividly that Heather and I had both said, "Lord where you will lead, we will go."

Once again God was going to surprise me. I went to fulfil a speaking engagement in Dunseverick Baptist Tabernacle along the beautiful North Antrim Coast. When I took the pulpit and began to preach I looked over the small, sparse congregation that seemed so discouraged and disillusioned. The Holy Spirit spoke to my heart and whispered softly, "this is my people, feed my sheep, this is where you will be." I came out of the service and sat in the car and phoned my wife with these words, "Pet we are going to be in Dunseverick."

We mentioned it to no one and left it with God, and sure enough the next Sunday that I was there, an office bearer asked if I was in a position to think before God about going into the work of God full time. My answer was simple, "You pray, and we will pray, and God will do the leading."

After much prayer and clear direction from the Bible and a formal call from the Church we met with The Rescue and informed them with a mixture of, sadness that we were leaving them and excitement that God was leading us into a new vineyard, of our decision to accept the call to the pastorate of Dunseverick Baptist Tabernacle.

But God had not finished with the surprises yet. You recall my brother Andrew? Heather was finishing her last shift in the Tesco store, she arrived home around 11:20pm and walked into the living room, I was sitting looking intently at my mobile phone and she inquired, "Why?" I responded with this, "Andrew is going to ring anytime soon and tell me that he has accepted Christ." Just a few minutes later the following word dialled up on my screen, 'bro'. I pressed the green receive button and said, "Hello Andrew, you're phoning to tell me you have accepted Christ." There was a short pause and then came the reply I had been waiting on for a very long time. Andrew was a rebellious, bad tempered, stubborn young man, "Yes Marc, I got saved just a few minutes ago in my bedroom." God you are faithful!!

November 2009, Heather, Dillon, Luke and I make the move to the North Coast to begin working amongst a different group of people but with the same message of a risen Saviour who not only died on a cross to reconcile them to God but who wanted to live within the people who called upon Him for salvation.

What a joy it was to be the bondservant of the Lord in Dunseverick Baptist Tabernacle, so many families reached with the gospel, so many lives altered for eternity, so many young people willing to step out of the comfort zone and serve the Lord. Yet, within the recesses of my soul, I still felt there was more to be accomplished for Christ, no matter how good a crowd came to the gospel service on a Sunday night I still knew that a big majority of the folk needing Christ were outside the four walls. The Spirit of the Lord was stirring the nest again and I increasingly found myself greater burdened with 'playing church', when outside the majority of people were lost and needed someone to tell them about the love of Christ. I began to pray this prayer that I had read and could not remember where but I had written this in front of my Bible:

"Lord, use me. Make me a soul winner. Send me out as an Evangelist. Let me see revival. Do not let me settle down in an ordinary pastorate and accomplish nothing. I have only one life and I want to invest it for You. Let me live and love others, enable me to win lost men and women and young people for whom You died and rose and want to live in. Let your blessing rest upon this ministry. Amen".

The question came foremost to our minds again, "Lord what will you have us do?" I sat for hours on end in the study before God, burdened deeply about the huge need. How was it that the world was doing everything possible to entice people into it and yet the church was doing everything possible to entice people away from it? The hunger for souls seemed to have evaporated from most believers, a theology of 'whoever is going to be saved will be saved' was sweeping through the country but yet here I was sitting with the infallible, inerrant, inspired Word of God and it was saying, *"Go into all the world and preach the good news to all creation..." (Mark 16:15).* Had the Great Commission changed? Where we to sit in our comfy, cosy church buildings and stay in a 'holy huddle' and let men and women perish who should be hearing the gospel? I knew the answer profoundly to that, the great commission has not changed one iota and the scripture was clear. *How, then, can they call on the one they have not believed in? And how can they believe in the one of whom they have not heard? And how can they hear without someone preaching to them? (Romans 10:14).*

So the Lord once again had brought to our attention the work of my dear friend and brother in the Lord, Mr. Ricky Bell and his dear wife Joyce who had commenced The Gospel Bus Ministry with an old Ulsterbus fully equipped to take the gospel to the people. I admired this brother so much, I loved his passion for the lost, I loved the fact that he was 'a man of faith.' Was it possible that the Lord could use us for something similar across the North Coast? How could we afford a bus? How would it succeed? Questions I should never and need never to worry about if God is in it.

My first meeting with Translink, well to say it was interesting was an understatement! I was laughed at and told in no uncertain terms that the idea was 'crazy' as was my friend Ricky also told a this at the time he had went to inquire, but yet I left the building and prayed earnestly as I drove up the motorway, "Lord only You can open this door, those men think it is impossible, but you love the impossible and You are the God of the impossible." No sooner had I said, "Amen," than my phone rang and at the other end one of the men from Translink who said, "I think that is a good idea, come back and pick your bus, we will sell you one." (It is not always that my prayers are answered as quickly as that but I shouted, "Hallelujah," that this time it was immediate).

The bus was purchased with money we had got from the sale of our family car, it was taken to a shed where huge renovation was soon to commence, but I knew in my heart that God was going to do something special and so He did. Gillian Millar, a nurse and a close friend of our family, a girl who had a heart for people, a love for souls and a fervent love for Christ, was the young lady along with her then boyfriend (now husband),David Stewart who were going to transform this bus. The determination, drive and passion that these two individuals showed was truly remarkable, Gillian spent long hours under the bus, on the bus, and in the bus working so selflessly. It was during this period of time that my attention was unexpectedly going to be diverted in two massive ways that would rock our family, test our faith and ultimately make us even more reliant on God. The next chapter will go into more detail on that, but for now I feel we should have another Selah and see what the Bible teaches us practically about how we should see the world the way Jesus sees it, through His eyes.

David while hiding in a cave said this, ***Look to my right and see; no one is concerned for me. I have no refuge; no one cares for my life (Psalm142:4).*** How sad the plight is, if not one of us cares for the soul of another, the passion that Jesus had, brought Him from Heaven to earth on a special rescue mission to save mankind. The whole purpose of the Lord Jesus Christ being born was actually to die for you and me, Jesus could say, ***"Just as the Father knows me and I know the Father – and I lay down my life for the sheep" (John 10:15).***

When you turn to the gospel of Matthew and I would like to lift this passage out once again from the King James Version, you can see clearly how Jesus felt and viewed the people, ***But when he saw the multitudes, he was moved with compassion on them, because they fainted, and were scattered abroad, as sheep having no shepherd (Matthew 9:36).***

There are five things that burdened the Lord Jesus Christ that ought to burden every Christian. This is what Christ saw as He surveyed the masses that thronged around Him:

* Jesus Saw They Were Scattered - ***We all, like sheep, have gone astray, each of us has turned to his own way; and the Lord has laid on him the iniquity of us all (Isaiah 53:6).***

   Do you ever notice how often the Lord Jesus used the illustration of sheep to describe sinners? Here in this passage the Lord Jesus views the people as sheep yet again. If you work with sheep you know exactly what I am talking about, sheep wander and when they are away from the care of the shepherd they do not do well on their own. Do you and I really understand that the majority of the world and the majority of our friends are away from God? If you are not a Christian then Jesus views you as scattered, maybe you feel that you are isolated and all alone and you can say like the Psalmist in Psalm142 vs.4 "no man cares for your soul." There is hope and blessing for you if that is how you feel. In Luke chapter 15 vs.3-7, the story is of one sheep that was of so much importance to the Shepherd that he leaves the ninety nine of his other sheep and goes after the one that is lost and when He finds it he places it on His shoulders rejoicing that He has found just the one lost sheep. You know what I love, please understand this, Jesus Christ is interested in just one, He must needs pass through Samaria to find a women, just one, that society had rejected and religion had refused as told in John 4. He stopped at the foot of a sycamore tree just to tell Zacchaeus to "make haste and come down," Luke 19 just one person, He is interested in the individual, He is interested in you, I could go on and on with illustrations, Jesus Christ sees you as scattered but He loves you and He longs to be your Shepherd.

- Jesus Saw They Were Sinful – *Therefore, just as sin entered the world through one man, and death through sin, and in this way death came to all men, because all have sinned - (Romans 5:12).*

There is a word in Matthew 9 vs.36 that you and I would recognise and use it in the context of someone who has **'passed out or swooned'** it is the word **'fainted.'** Can I give you the true meaning of that word as Jesus saw these people, He saw them hopeless, helpless and weighed down beneath a burden of sin. This world and the people in it are sinful, the reality is that what we hear on the news headlines hardly bothers us anymore. How low is man going to stoop before God intervenes? What Dad takes his daughter in the car and abuses her? What man can pour acid over his girlfriend's body in a fit of jealous rage and scars her for life? This world is sinful and it is sinking lower and lower into the depths of depravity and we really do not know what we are going to hear next.

- Jesus Saw That They Were Sentenced – *Whoever believes in him is not condemned, but whoever does not believe stands condemned already because he has not believed in the name of God's one and only Son (John 3:18).*

I sat and I read this over and over again to myself and thought why Jesus was moved with compassion. Do you know why? As He looked at this mass of people, scattered and sinful, Jesus knew the end from the beginning and knew that some of them had a sentence of hell and the lake of fire hanging over their heads. I know that some of you are immediately thinking, well if Jesus was moved with compassion and Jesus is God then why can He not just take everyone to Heaven and send no one to hell and then everything will be sorted. Let me give you 2 verses, *The Lord is not slow in keeping his promise, as some understand slowness. He is patient with you, not wanting anyone to perish, but everyone to come to repentance (2ⁿᵈ Peter 3:9).* There is a responsibility on you and me as individuals to call, *For, "Everyone who calls on the name of the Lord will be saved (Romans 10:13).* We need to be sensitive and very clear about this because this subject causes massive problems to so many people, God did not hand pick a certain few and say when they were born, "Well I am going to choose him but not his sister or vice versa." But what God knows are those who are chosen before the world began, God knows the end from the beginning. God alone knows those who are going to call out to Him for salvation and every man, woman boy and girl can do so but there are those who will refuse and God knows that and as Jesus looked upon this huge crowd of people He knew that some of them would not choose Him and the sentence was already passed upon them. Christian we believe in hell, we talk about hell we thank God that we are not going to be in hell but if we really got just a two second vision of what it is like to be in hell and had our kingdom glasses on and saw things through Jesus' eyes would we not be moved with compassion to tell others about Jesus? You know what shakes me to the very core, there are people in hell right now and they are more concerned about the lost around us than some of us Christians are ourselves. *"He answered, 'Then I beg you, father, send Lazarus to my father's house, for I have five brothers. Let them warn them, so that they will not also come to this place of torment' (Luke 16:27).*

• Jesus Saw They Were **S**pecial – *For you are a people holy to the Lord your God, The Lord your God has chosen you out of all the peoples on the face of the earth to be his people, his treasured possession (Deuteronomy 7:6).*

As Jesus is moved with compassion and looks at the people, he speaks to His disciples and He tells them that the harvest is absolutely huge. As I look at this I can almost see Jesus looking at the crowd as individuals and seeing every single person as special. I love this, it totally thrills me when I think about it, 'Jesus thinks I'm special.' Oh in a society where people are made to feel completely worthless and people feel useless, Jesus looks on them and He says "You are special." *"Before I formed you in the womb I knew you, before you were born I set you apart; I appointed you as prophet to the nations" (Jeremiah 1:5).*

- Jesus Saw They Needed Servants – *Then I heard the voice of the Lord saying, "Whom shall I send? And who will go for us?" (Isaiah 6:8).*

Why is it that we Christians always talk about being saved from the three P's. We believe that we are saved from the Power of Sin, we believe that we are saved from the Penalty of Sin and we believe with all of our hearts that one day we will be saved from the very Presence of Sin and these are all true. But I have learnt an important truth from scripture that sadly has taken me many years to understand, it is not just about being 'saved from,' but equally as important is what also we are 'saved for', *For we are God's workmanship, created in Christ Jesus to do good works, which God prepared in advance for us to do so (Ephesians 2:10).* I want to be faithful to all of you who say you are saved, if you are doing nothing for Jesus then you are in the group that says 'saved from,' if you are excited and He has revealed Himself to you in a new way and you see things differently then you are in the group which is asking, "What am I saved for?"

God, speak to me, reveal to me Your heart, let me see things in a new perspective, the way You see things. I have settled down and become content in my own life, I need to step out of this comfort zone, I long for that hunger and the passion to win souls You have died for. Please give me a fresh glimpse of Calvary and the finished work, show me the empty tomb, and teach me what it means to love as You love. I thank You there is hope for everyone who calls upon Your name in faith, in Jesus name, Amen.

CHAPTER EIGHT

BATTLES

1Pe 1:7 These have come so that your faith – of greater worth than gold, which perishes even though refined by fire – may be proved genuine and may result in praise, glory and honor when Jesus Christ is revealed. Though you have not seen him, you love him; and even though you do not see him now, you believe in him and are filled with an inexpressible and glorious joy, for you are receiving the goal of your faith, the salvation of your souls.

One of my favourite singers of all time is Lynda Randle, time and time again I listen to one song in particular, 'God of The Mountain'.

Life is easy, when you're up on the mountain
And you've got peace of mind, like you've never known
But things change, when you're down in the valley
Don't lose faith, for your never alone
Chorus: For the God on the mountain, is still God in the valley
When things go wrong, he'll make them right
And the God of the good times, is still God in the bad times
The God of the day, is still God in the night
We talk of faith way up on the mountain
But talk comes easy, when life's at its best
Now it's down in the valleys, trials and temptations
That's where your faith is really put to the test
Chorus: For the God on the mountain, is still God in the valley,
When things go wrong, he'll make them right

And the God of the good times, is still God in the bad times
The God of the day, is still God in the night
The God of the day, is still God in the night

Dunseverick Baptist, the bus and various missions over the country, I was truly on the mountain top, God was blessing and the Christian life was exciting, there were hiccups yes, but nothing that seemed to perturb us. I should have been spiritually mature enough to understand that the enemy was always sure to attack after victories. However I was completely oblivious as to how and where the enemy was going to attack, it was going to come in a three pronged attack but with one solitary goal........ family!

My sister had a marriage break-up, since that time she had struggled immensely mentally, many times there were hospitalisations and many times I had received phone calls from my mother who was so burdened about her daughter and who felt so powerless to do anything that would relive her suffering. My mother has been ill for many years with M.E, that serious paralyzing Chronic Fatigue Syndrome. We had watched a vibrant, energetic mother who had worked two jobs and cared for four kids, dramatically lose weight and rapidly become only a shadow of the woman she once was, the strain on my mother of one of her children's marriages breaking down was taking its toll.

My brother took a lot of the responsibility helping my sister out, but he was a new Christian. I was long enough down the Christian pathway now to know the card the devil would play, "Some God you have, look at the way He has left your mum and now your sister." The 'accuser of the brethren' the enemy never stops, he cannot get the believer and rob them of salvation but he certainly will try and stop their joy and fellowship and communion with God.

My sister suffered terribly, everything that a mental affliction can bring she was enduring, this was my sister, the one who, when we were growing up adapted a fantastic motherly role with us especially when mum took ill. This was my sister the one who came out to the playing pitches and found it no problem at all to play a football match with the boys from the estate. What I was observing now was not the sister I knew. No matter how many hospitalisations and how many pills and 'doctors reports' and 'labels', I was uneasy, I was not convinced that what they said and the labels placed upon the illness was true. Now please do not get me wrong, I do believe in mental illness I have observed it with my mother-in-law and now in my sister. But in my mind and heart and as I sat before God and studied the scripture, I was convinced that a big majority of psychologists had only a natural world view on illness that did not include a spiritual Godly view

It was evident to me that depression was a threefold illness, it affected the body, i.e. headaches, nausea, tiredness, it was also a soul matter, and it was also a spirit matter, and if that being the case, then it needed a body, soul and spirit response to the problem. As I looked at my sister, so often my mind was drawn to scripture, in the Bible a mental affliction was associated with demonic attack, today of course we call it all sorts of medical names, the problem however arises because the majority of evangelical Christians will jump down your throat when you put demonic attack and believer in the same sentence. But why? Look at scripture, any time there was demonic oppression or demons it was associated with things like, self-harming and suicidal thoughts (Mark 5). When this man is delivered the very first things that the demons do when they enter the pigs is to cause them all to take their lives by running violently over the cliff edge. Everything that I read in scripture in relation to demonic attack was observed in every symptom of my sister.

Paul wrote, **For our struggle is not against flesh and blood, but against the rulers, against the authorities, against the powers of this dark world and against the spiritual forces of evil in heavenly realms (Ephesians 6:12).** For some apparent reason many evangelical believers claim 'life on other planets', like

Neptune or Uranus are the 'heavenly realms' mentioned in this verse. When Paul talks about **"the heavenly realms,"** the word is **"epouranios,"** pronounced **"ep-oo-ran'-ee-os"** which means **'above the sky:--celestial, (in) heaven(-ly), high.'** It is here, now, that we believers wrestle against the demonic attacks. Satan is the **"*god of this world, the prince of the power of the air*"** *(Ephesians 2:2).*

As I have previously mentioned in past chapters, there is a battle of deception, a battle for the mind, it has been here since the beginning of time, it should not come as a surprise to us. From Genesis to Revelation the battle is clear. It is a battle between Christ and the anti christ (Satan), and the tool Satan uses is always and will always be deception, if he can get a believer to believe a lie like he did with Eve in the Garden of Eden, look closely at this verse once more, ***Now the serpent was more crafty than any of the wild animals the Lord God had made. He said to the woman, "Did God really say, 'You must not eat from any tree in the garden'?" (Genesis 3:1).*** Then when the lie is sown and we latch on to the lie and believe it, we turn away from the truth. How do we know when we turn away from the truth? The answer to that is simple, many who struggle mentally suffer from a terrible thing called fear, now fear is not from God, how can it be because we know what God has given to the believer, ***For God did not give us a spirit of timidity, but a spirit of power, of love and of self-discipline (2Timothy 1:7).*** Yet within all phobias the key element that is at the heart of the very problem is fear. Of course fear breeds fear, and before long the fear of fear itself is the eventual outcome.

Again, take a look at scripture with me on this, here is what Christ said to His apostles, ***When Jesus had called the Twelve together, he gave them power and authority to drive out all demons and to cure diseases (Luke 9:1).*** The important truth to take notice of here, is the fact that the Lord Jesus had not been to the cross as yet. At this time of giving the apostles this empowering anointing, Satan had not been defeated, that meant that believers were not seated with Christ in the 'heavenly places'. But that was all going to change at Calvary and in the power of Christ's resurrection, you see these two very special events were going to expose who Satan was and disarm him completely and permanently, furthermore look at what Jesus Himself said, *Then Jesus came to them and said, "All authority in heaven and on earth has been given to me (Matthew 28:18).* Grasp this truth with both hands, because **"all power, all authority"** has been given to Christ and everyone that believes in Him are alive and seated with Christ in heavenly places, *But because of his great love for us, God, who is rich in mercy, made us alive with Christ even when we were dead in transgressions – it is by grace you have been saved. And God raised us up with Christ, and seated us with him in the heavenly realms in Christ Jesus, in order that in the coming ages he might show the incomparable riches of his grace, expressed in his kindness to us in Christ Jesus. For it is by grace you have been saved, through faith – and this not from yourselves, it is the gift of God – not by works, so that no one can boast (Ephesians 2:4-9).* The truth is this, you and I as believers do not need to defeat Satan, Christ has already accomplished that, all you have do to is "by grace, through faith" receive that truth.

When the enemy gets a foothold and when you give him an inch, he will take a mile. I was beginning to understand something of the truths of scripture that, yet, once again I had been taught nothing of as I was growing up as a young Christian, deliverance was needed, demons needed to be cast out, wounds needed to be healed and sin needed to be repented of. Many evangelical believers today live in some 'spiritual cocoon' in which they believe that the devil and his countless myriads of demons cannot touch them, perish this erroneous man made doctrine, every single Christian at the moment of salvation enters into spiritual battlefield not a spiritual playingfield. To observe anyone who suffers with mental illness is disturbing and upsetting, but when it is within the boundaries of your own immediate family it has an impact that can only be described as devastating. I do not wish to go into great detail in this book with regards to many of the things that we as a family have witnessed in relation to my sister because so much of it is disturbing and will revive past memories. However, what I do want to reiterate is this, what we observed was not my sister, there was and had to be some outside dark influence and that scripturally can only be the devil and his demons.

June 2011, Heather and I attended an appointment at The Royal Victoria Hospital, unknown to many Heather had been struggling for years with severe Endometriosis. (Endometriosis is the abnormal growth of cells (endometrial cells) similar to those that form the inside of the uterus, but in a location outside of the uterus. Endometrial cells are cells that are shed each month during menstruation. The cells of endometriosis attach themselves to tissue outside the uterus and are called endometriosis implants. These implants are most commonly found on the ovaries, the Fallopian tubes, outer surfaces of the uterus or intestines, and on the surface lining of the pelvic cavity).

After scans we attended for the results, the news was bleak, Heather needed major surgery, endometriosis had completely taken over her abdomen, her bowel, ovaries and womb had all been affected. In the Consultants opinion he felt we should go home and think over it especially because of the risks and complications that would be associated with the surgery. I thought within myself, that's good, we will go home and talk it over and think on it, but Heather immediately replied, "I will take the surgery, I cannot continue to live like this, I have to try this surgery."

Surgery was arranged and it was during this period of waiting that attack two was going to come. Our youngest son Luke began to become isolated and his appetite became affected, before long he was neither eating or taking on fluids, he cried himself to sleep night after night with both Heather and me beside him. It was heart wrenching to us as parents to watch this. What had happened? Had we done something wrong? Where was God now, why me? All were questions that engulfed us. We knew if he did not eat and did not drink before long he would be hospitalised, and so it was that he was admitted to the Causeway Hospital. The diagnosis, Severe Obsessive Compulsive Disorder, or dare I say it, a battle for the mind even in a ten year old who had trusted Christ and was very sincere and very devoted in following Him. The next few weeks and months were horrendous, we can empathise with parents who have or who are presently in the midst of such a trial with one of their children. So many afflictions are engulfing our children in these days, bulimia, anorexia, ADHD and anxiety disorders to name but a few. These all originate in the mind but with them come in many instances physical symptoms. As parents we faced the meetings with social workers, physciatrists and doctors, the scrutiny on our parenting which brought us much pain. We appreciated that these specialists were observing and bringing a diagnosis from a 'worldview' but within our hearts as parents we recognised this from a spiritual perspective. We claimed the truth and understood that victory was already won by Christ. Through much pray from so many of God's people throughout the world Luke returned to full health. To God be the Glory.

September 2011, Heather is taken into the Royal Victoria Hospital for her surgery, I pray with her as she is wheeled away to theatre, "God we are cast upon You, we know that You created this body, because you remember that we are dust, please guide the hands of the surgeons and bring Heather through."

The day seemed like a year, but at 5:30pm I got the call to say Heather was returning to the ward. As I made my way up in the elevator I wondered had she needed a colostomy bag, was the surgery successful, what now? Heather opened her eyes when I appeared and her first words were, "No bag." This news thrilled us both and we thanked God from our hearts.

The following week I brought our two boys Dillon and Luke down to see their mum, Heather had been given the news that she would be discharged the following day. As we left hospital and looked up from the car park at Heather waving, we were overjoyed, mum was coming home, or as the boys like to think of her, 'the roof was going back on our family home'.But sadly on the day that we were to bring Heather home the outlook was not as bright, Heather had taken ill and was to remain in hospital for a further two weeks.

After this very trying period Heather was discharged and we came home but something was just not right. We understood very well that Heather had major surgery, and yes I knew it was not going to be an immediate recovery, but there was something wrong, it was only a matter of days before Heather was readmitted to hospital.

It was soon discovered that as a result of the surgery, Heather had developed a stricture in her bowel. She needed more major surgery and sooner rather than later but the surgeons were gravely concerned that it was 'too soon' after her first surgery.

So it was decided that in spite of the fact that the amazing surgeon who cared for Heather in The Royal Victoria Hospital felt it was risky to operate so soon after the first operation there was no other alternative, there had to be further surgery, and it could not wait, it had to be now. When Heather again returned from surgery we soon were informed that an illestomy bag was needed. Heather adapted to this change magnificently but things were still not going to be straight forward and clear cut.

After surgery and the initial first few days that seemed to go fine in recovery Heather deteriorated rapidly. I recall one particular Thursday so vividly when Heather was extremely poor, and our dear friends Pastor Kenneth Humphries and his wife Isa who had been so faithful in their ministry to us at this time, were sitting at the bedside. We all knew that something had to give.

Another dear friend Raymond McDowell arrived at the hospital and as they wheeled Heather away to theatre for the fourth time, Raymond wept. He had watched his own dear wife Adrienne die of cancer. I asked him one straightforward question, "Raymond do you think I could lose Heather?" I knew the answer but I wanted to hear the truth, "Yes" he replied. Raymond prayed with me, God had sent once again His servant to minister at the exact time I needed.

I arrived home about 1:20am. I opened the kitchen door, fell prostrate on my face and cried, "God, I am desperate for You, I need You, You have to take over here, please just let me see Heather smile." Through my tears I mumbled the words, I hardly knew how to pray or what to pray, but I did not care because I knew the Word of God said, *In the same way, the Spirit helps us in our weakness. We do not know what we ought to pray for, but the Spirit himself intercedes for us with groans that words cannot express. And he who searches our hearts knows the mind of the Spirit, because the Spirit intercedes for the saints in accordance with God's will. And we know that in all things God works for the good of those who love him, who have been called according to his purpose (Romans 8:26-28).* So often we are bombarded with bad news and in the intensity of the heat of the moment we are left bewildered and overwhelmed by what we have to face. When you can not find words to say understand that the Lord of glory observes every tear that falls, *You know my wanderings: put thou my tears into thy bottle: are they not in thy book? (Psalm 56:8).*

The following morning I arrived at the hospital at ten past eleven, I knew that visiting was strictly two until four pm but I needed to be there. As I walked the corridor to ward 6A I was met by the sister in charge who said, "You are going to be a happy man this morning." I nearly burst through the ward doors, there was Heather sitting up on the bed with two pillow props smiling!!! Yes she had needed an illestomy, yes the recuperation period was going to be lengthy but God had brought her through. He said it and I believed it, *'Call to Me, and I will answer you and tell you great and unsearchable things you do not know (Jeremiah 33:3)*

You recall one of my questions was, Why me? Well it was during this period of time that I personally needed to take the time and have a Selah. God showed me something completely different and it was special, the question "Why me"? Was dramatically changed around to a different question, "Why **NOT** me?"

I have often thought about Carson McCullers, the novelist, maybe some of you have never read or heard about her. The question was once asked of Mrs McCullers, "How much suffering can one person bear?" To which a really unusual answer was given, "More." Mrs McCullers was described at her funeral service as a woman, "with a vocation of pain," it was said that much of her creative ability came about as a result of her own personal sufferings in life. Let me just share something about her life's experiences. Before she was 29 years old Mrs McCullers had suffered three strokes which left her paralyzed down the left side, she thought that she could never write again but she resumed her work by doing a page a day. The pain of three strokes grew rapidly day by day, her husband died by suicide and, in later years, she was left almost completely disabled. She seldom talked about her troubles but on one very rare occasion she was asked "Do you never ask God why? To which she replied, "Sometimes I do think that God got me mixed up with Job but Job never cursed God and neither have I, I just carry on."

We all have our 'why' moments in life, do we not? In February 15th 1947 a man by the name of Glenn Chambers boarded a plane to commence missionary work in Quito, Ecuador, he never got to Quito because the plane on which he travelled crashed into a mountain and dropped to the ground. It was later learned that before he left Miami airport Glenn had tried to find some paper to write his mum a letter and in a state of rushing to board the plane the only thing he found was an advertising leaflet with one solitary word written in the middle of it, "Why?" He added his own personal message to his mum on the reverse side and days after Glenn's death the letter which he had written arrived at his home, on opening the envelope his mother took out the paper to behold one word, "Why?"

I am aware that most preachers will say that in suffering we should never question God, and to a point I agree with that but can I say that I believe with all of my heart that there is nothing scripturally wrong with asking God the question, "why?" Can I suggest to you that there are times when the answer will not be given in this life but there are other times when God will show you quite clearly the plans and the purposes. Be assured of this one thing that God is working things out for your Eternal Good and for His Eternal Glory. Remember what the Lord Himself uttered on the cross, *From the sixth hour until the ninth hour darkness came over all the land. About the ninth hour Jesus cried out in a loud voice, "Eloi, Eloi, lama sabachthani?" which means, "My God ,my God, why have you forsaken me?" (Matthew 27:46).*

Yes certainly we can ask "Why?" about a lot of things in life, Why is it that the good always suffer? Why is it that some children have to die of starvation while others have so much? Why? Why? Why? Life is full of these why moments, but can we the change 'Why me?' as God, through the Holy Spirit changed it in my life, to "Why Not Me?" once again I have chosen the King James Version to look in some detail at Job and the events and challenges that he faced.

- Job And His **A**dversities

  When you read the opening chapter of the book of Job there are some notable things that I want to point out. In verse 6 you will read *Now there was a day when the sons of God came to present themselves before the LORD, and Satan came also among them (Job 1:6).* There are regular days when angels come to worship in Heaven, sometimes we think that we are the only ones on planet earth that are involved in worship, but not so. Please remember these verses, *For by him all things were created: things in heaven and on earth, visible and invisible, whether thrones or powers or rulers or authorities; all things were created by him and for him. He is before all things, and in him all things hold together (Colossians 1:16-17).*Where there is intelligent life there is intelligent worship. Let me also point this out as well, Satan has access into Heaven, many younger believers seem to think that Satan is sending forth his orders from hell but that is far from the truth, Satan is not in hell in fact we read, *In which you used to live when you followed the ways of this world and of the ruler of the kingdom of the air, the spirit who is now at work in those who are disobedient (Ephesians 2:2).* We can also read, *The god of this age has blinded the minds of unbelievers, so that they cannot see the light of the gospel of the glory of Christ, who is the image of God (2Corinthians 4:4).* Satan has access into Heaven. In Job 1 vs.1, many people have lifted out the word **"perfect"** and started a whole debate on sinless perfection because it says that Job was **"perfect."** Let me point out that the word used here in relation to **"perfect"** is the word **"tam,"** pronounced **"tawn"** which relates to his integrity. So what was the secret to Job's perfect or straight integrity? Simply this "he feared God." The word **"feared"** here is the word **"yare"** pronounced **"yaw-ray,"** it means complete awe and reverence. Let me give you this little quotation so we can really grasp what it is to fear God.

"The remarkable thing about fearing God, is that when you fear God you fear nothing else, whereas if you don't fear God you fear everything else." ('My Utmost For His Highest' by Oswald Chambers).

Let us look at the Adversities Job faced:

(i) **Farm** – Initially a servant comes to say that the Sabeans had attacked and had carried away Job's cows and his donkeys and killed all his farm labourers there except the one that came to tell him the news. Now let me just put this into some perspective. With this first adversity that Job faced, in Job 1:3 you will notice that he had 500 yoke of oxen and 500 she asses. So the value of the first loss was 1,000 cows at $325 a cow which was $325,000. Then notice please the use of the reference to 'she asses' they were worth far more than the male because of the milk they produced, so 500 she asses at a value of $50 amounted to $25,000 . Then another servant comes while the first servant is just finishing, with his news to say that the fire of God had fallen. Can I suggest to you that this fire could very well have been a lightning storm as even today many believe that storms come as a result of God's anger. Here the sheep are destroyed and Job had 7,000 of them at $20 a head which was a total of $140,000 dollars lost. Then, as this servant is speaking, another comes to say that the Chaldeans had taken away the camels, killed the farm labourers and this messenger was the only one left to tell the news. There were 3,000 camels at $100 a camel which amounted to $300,000.

By using the comparison against US dollars, someone has arrived at the following figures which I found to be staggering.

1,000 @ $325 = $325,000
500 she asses @ $50 = $25,000
7,000 sheep @ $20 = $140,000
3,000 camels @$100 = $300,000

Total loss = $790,000

(ii) **Family** – Just when Job thinks he has heard it all, another man comes to tell Job that while his 10 children were all in the oldest child's house, a great hurricane or tornado came and the house had fallen and killed everyone of them.

(iii) Fitness – You would think in light of all that Job has lost so far that he would start to really have a shaky faith and question God but the very last verse of chapter 1 tells us differently, *In all this Job sinned not, nor charged God foolishly (Job 1:22).* Chapter 2 commences with Satan again in Heaven, this time Job is going to face a different adversity and it is going to hit his body. In verse 7 we read that Job is struck down with boils. The word **"boils"** here is **"Shechiyn,"** this is like a festering tumour that was an extreme swelling and pussing sore, it was described to me as elephantiasis which is disfigurement so severe that the person is unrecognisable.

(iv) Friends – So often when we are faced with extreme difficulty and when our backs are against the wall it is then we can really see who our real friends are. Job had friends but when he needed them most they let him down. I am reminded so often what Paul said, *At my first defense, no one came to my support, but everyone deserted me. May it not be held against them. But the Lord stood at my side and gave me strength, so that through me the message might be fully proclaimed and all the Gentiles might hear it. And I was delivered from the lion's mouth (2nd Timothy 4:16-17).*

What Adversities are you facing just now? There are none of us who are exempt from them, *"I have told you these things, so that in me you may have peace. In this world you will have trouble. But take heart! I have overcome the world (.John 16:33).*

Adversities in life can do one of two things; they can either make you **Lean** or make you **Lament.**

• Job And His **A**llies

We have all heard of that expression in life 'Job's Comforters.' In chapter 2 verse 11 we read that Job's allies come to do two things, mourn with him and comfort him. The word **"comfort"** here is the word **"nacham"** pronounced **"naw-kham"** it simply means to console or take pity or sympathise. Sadly, despite the very thing that allies are meant to do, Job's allies actually did the complete opposite. You know the sure test of true friends really comes in the midst of suffering, you can tell so much about their spirituality and the general character of them during difficult times. Let us look at Job's friends now.

(i) **Eliphaz** – The **P**essimistic Man – this is one of those men who has 'been there done that and got the T-shirt,' only what he has been through is far worse than you will ever be through, sounds familiar doesn't it? There are two things I notice in the four chapters that this man uses when speaking, chapter 4, 5, 15, 22.

   (a) He **B**utters Job Up – Chapter 4 vs.3-4 he comes initially and tells Job how great an encouragement he has been to others but it soon changes.

   (b) He **B**eats Job Up – Chapter 4 vs.5-11 he says to Job that really Job is a hypocrite vs.8, weakling vs.5-6, and a wicked person vs.10-11.

(ii) **Bildad** – The **P**rivileged Man – this man is one of those people who has had a fairly easy run in life. They have never been in a situation that is severe so therefore they see things in a very clear picture and that is, 'life is what you make of it yourself.' How you establish yourself in life will be how it turns out for you. I noticed two distinct things that Bildad says that the exact same type of people will say today also: Bildad takes three chapters to have his say, 8, 18, 25.

(a) He Calls Job A **Wh**inge – chapter 8 vs.2

(b) He Calls Job **W**icked - chapter 8 verses 3-22

(iii) **Zophar** – The **P**ious Man - this man just tells Job that he is far away from God and needs to get his life with God right, in fact when you read chapter 11 he tells Job that he has got far less than he actually deserved. He takes up 2 chapters of the book, 11 & 20. There were two characteristics that I notice he brought to the situation:

(a) **H**yper **H**oliness- This man really says that you are only in this situation if you are not right with God. I have met so many believers like this in my Christian walk, they seem to feel because they have never had any battles in their lives that those who suffer or get it tough must not be walking closely with God. That may be the case in SOME situations but certainly in my experiences not them all. I have known many believers who 'walked with God' just like Enoch and they have experienced some of the most horrendous heartbreaks you could ever imagine.

(b) **H**alf **H**earted Friendship – This man actually took a bit of delight in the fact that he, himself, seems to be holy and that Job seems to need rebuked by God.

(iv) **Elihu** – The **P**roud Man – There is always one of these people everywhere, they sit back and wait and listen to everyone and then they pounce and come with the general phrase, "No harm to you all, every one of you is wrong, this is the right way of it." Again I noticed two things about him that he brought to the situation.

(a) **I**nexperience – When you read chapter 32 verses 6+7 you will notice that he is just young. He has not experienced in life anything to the extent that Job has.

(b) **I**neffectiveness – It takes this man five whole chapters
to say that God is so Good chapters 32, 33, 34,
35,36 but the whole purpose in his long windedness
absolutely brings no comfort to Job and no good to
the situation. What he says contained some powerful
material but his method of explanation and delivery
was all wrong.

Remember this, *Wounds from a friend can be trusted, but
an enemy multiplies kisses (Proverbs 27:6).* There is no
harm whatsoever in a true friend coming and warning us and
pointing out faults. I referred to Nathan the prophet earlier
how that he pointed out to David the sin into which he had
fallen. The problem that arises however is when 'friends' come
with premeditated motives to 'stick the knife in further'.

- Job And His **A**ttitude –

It would have been very easy for Job just to say like his wife, "
*Dost thou still retain thine integrity? curse God, and die"
(Job 2:9).* It is so easy in times of suffering, loss and grief to
turn it around and blame God, but we must always try and
see the bigger picture. The trials are not to **P**ush you over the
Precipice, in fact the trails are to **P**erfect our **P**athway. I have
learnt so much from the attitude of Job let me share some key
things from this:

(a) He **P**rayed - *Then Job arose, and rent his mantle, and
shaved his head, and fell down upon the ground, and
worshipped, (Job 1:20).* We sing it so often:

Have we trials and temptations?
Is there trouble anywhere?
We should never be discouraged:
Take it to the Lord in prayer!

It is one thing singing it; it is another thing putting it into practice.

(a) He **P**roclaimed - *And said, Naked came I out of my mother's womb, and naked shall I return thither: the LORD gave, and the LORD hath taken away; blessed be the name of the LORD (Job 1:21).* This is what I found really amazing, after everything that Job lost he is proclaiming that his faith in God has remained the same. How easy it is to say," Blessed be the name of the Lord," when something fantastic has happened in your life but to say it when you have just lost something precious to you..........that's a challenge!

(b) He **P**ondered - *But he said unto her, Thou speakest as one of the foolish women speaketh. What? shall we receive good at the hand of God, and shall we not receive evil? In all this did not Job sin with his lips (Job 2:10).* Job did not immediately rush in with accusations against God, he just pondered as to why this would all be happening.

(c) He **P**aused – Job waited on God and even though he could not get his head around it he knew that he had to just wait on God's timing, no better way to do it than the way Job did, he just fixed his eyes on God, *Job 42:5 I have heard of thee by the hearing of the ear: but now mine eye seeth thee (Job 42:5).*

This is the attitude we all need, in the face of adversity always keep in mind the verse, *For I know the plans I have for you, declares the Lord," "plans to prosper you and not to harm you, plans to give you hope and a future (Jeremiah 29:11*

- Job And His **A**ttainment –

At the end of it all, when the dust had settled so to speak, Job attained certain things out of the Adversities he faced. It is just wonderful that when through adversity that we face in life we can learn something and look back and see God's providence in it.

(a) His **A**wareness - *I know that thou canst do every thing, and that no thought can be withholden from thee (Job 42:2).* Job was eventually made aware that all of the things he faced were all to do with the glory of God, this is it in a nutshell. Everything in our Christian walk ultimately is about bringing God the glory, God wants to exalt His son in the situations that you and I face. *Whether therefore ye eat, or drink, or whatsoever ye do, do all to the glory of God (1ˢᵗ Corinthians 10:31).*

(b) His **A**ssets - *So the LORD blessed the latter end of Job more than his beginning: for he had fourteen thousand sheep, and six thousand camels, and a thousand yoke of oxen, and a thousand she asses (Job 42:12).* My dear believer, God is no man's debtor, God can give to you and give to me twice as much as we have lost or will ever loose.

(c) His **A**cknowledgement - *He had also seven sons and three daughters (Job 42:13).* I found it amazing that the Word of God records just here the names of the three daughters, but then the Word of God makes no mistakes and they are recorded for a specific purpose. Look at the three names of the daughters because I believe that in the names we see Job acknowledging a powerful God.

1. **Jemima** – The meaning of the name is **"Bright or Beautiful Day and Dove"** Oh, after the night of turmoil and suffering that Job endured he names his first daughter Jemima acknowledging that a new day had dawned, with fresh hope, fresh light and a fresh sense of peace as a dove is the symbol of rest.

2. **Kezia** – This comes from the herb **Cassia** bringing that sweet smell. *All thy garments smell of myrrh, and aloes, and cassia, out of the ivory palaces, whereby they have made thee glad (Ps 45:8).* Job is acknowledging that the bad smell of suffering and death has been replaced with the sweet smell of God's goodness.

3. **Keren –Happuch** – This name means **"beautifier or horn of paint."** Her name refers to a box of paint which was a vessel containing cosmetic liquids and fragrances and was frequently made of horn. You will recall when Moses came down of the mountain and there was that glow of his face, this is the picture behind this name meaning. Job in naming his third daughter acknowledges that when God comes, when His presence becomes a reality, the outward beauty with all of the blemishes is replaced by an inward beauty that God can give. In the end the glory of God is the ultimate concern, nothing else really matters.

God knows exactly where you are right now in life, *But He knows the way that I take; When He has tested me, I shall come forth as gold (Job 23:10).* It may seem presently so hopeless to you and it may appear that there is no way out. Keep believing, the Christian life is the call to a life of faith. When we can't figure things out, just faith it out. Can God take battles that we face in our Christian lives and bring something beautiful out of them? Of course He can, that is what God is all about. I love this story of encouragement in the midst of a great battle:

Ruby Hamilton, a businesswoman in her fifties, was stunned at the loss of her husband of 32 years in a car accident. Her anger and disappointment went deeper than a more typical expression of grief though. She had become a follower of Christ in her late twenties, but her husband didn't share her newfound interest in spiritual things. Nonetheless, she had set about praying for him feverishly and unceasingly that he would come to know the Lord. And one day when she was praying, she felt a wave of peace wash over her, and that still small voice assuring her that her husband would be okay. She eagerly awaited the day when her husband surrender his life to Jesus. And now this bombshell that her husband had died so tragically.

What do you do when faith doesn't make sense? When God doesn't seem to be answering or opening doors or being found? Ruby Hamilton stopped living for God.

Roger Simmons was hitchhiking his way home. He would never forget the date - May 7th. His heavy suitcase was making him tired and he was anxious to take off that army uniform once and for all. Flashing the thumb to the oncoming car, he lost hope when he saw it was a black, sleek new Cadillac. To his surprise the car stopped.

The passenger door swung open. He ran toward the car, tossed his suitcase in the back and thanked the handsome, well-dressed man as he slid into the front seat. "Going home for keeps?"

"Sure am."

"Well, you're in luck if you're going to Chicago."

"Not quite that far - do you live in Chicago?"

"I have a business there, the driver said. My name is Hamilton."

They chatted for a while, and then Roger, a Christian, felt a compulsion to share his faith with this fiftyish, apparently successful business man. But he kept putting it off, till he realized that he was now just 30 minutes from his home. It was now or never.

"Mr. Hamilton, I would like to talk to you about something very important." Then he simply told Mr. Hamilton about the plan of salvation and ultimately asked him if he would like to receive Jesus as his Saviour and Lord.

The Cadillac pulled over to the side of the road. Roger expected that he was about to get thrown out of the car. Instead, the businessman bowed his head and received Christ, then thanked Roger "This is the greatest thing that has ever happened to me."

Five years went by. Roger married, had a couple of kids and a business of his own. Packing his suitcase for a trip to Chicago he found a small white business card that had been given to him by Hamilton five years previous. In Chicago, he looked up Hamilton enterprises. The receptionist told him that it was impossible to see Mr. Hamilton, but he could see Mrs. Hamilton. A little confused, he was ushered into a beautiful office where he found himself facing a keen-eyed woman in her fifties.

She extended her hand "You knew my husband?"

Roger told her about how Hamilton had picked him up while he was hitchhiking home after the war. "Can you tell me what day that was?"

"Sure it was May 7th, five years ago, the day I was discharged from the army."

"Anything special about that day," she asked.

He hesitated, not knowing if he should mention how he shared the message of Jesus with her husband. "Mrs. Hamilton, I explained the gospel to your husband that day. He pulled over to the side of the road and wept against the steering wheel. He gave his life to Christ that day."

Explosive sobs shook her body. Finally getting a grip on herself, she sobbed, "I had prayed for my husband's salvation for years. I believed God would save him."

"Where is your husband, Ruby?"

"He's dead. He was in a car crash after he let you out of the car. He never got home. You see, I thought God had not kept his promise. I stopped living for God five years ago because I thought God had not kept his word!"

(Considerable influence for this message came from John Piper's "The Spring of Persistent Public Love", DesiringGod.org. From a sermon by Bret Toman, Power to Live the Golden Rule, 1/3/2011)

Father, I thank You so much that You alone know the end from the beginning, so many times in life we question things. I acknowledge that I am guilty so often of not claiming the truth and the promises of scripture, thank You for Your patience, Your mercy and Your grace. Help me to keep understanding the truth as Job understood it, that my Redeemer lives. Thank You for bringing us through the battles so that we can become more like Christ. In Jesus name, Amen.

CHAPTER NINE

BELIEVE

Isa 43:19 See, I am doing a new thing! Now it springs up; do you not perceive it? I am making a way in the desert and streams in the wasteland.

'Believe', a word that is paramount in the Christian faith but also used by many in the world as well. Without belief we will stumble and fall and never amount to anything whether that be in the physical realm or in the spiritual.

God was blessing in Dunseverick Baptist, folk were being saved and baptised and added to the local church. In the missions that I was engaged in outside the church work in Kilrea, Coagh, Soul Cafe in Drumreagh, Limavady and Preston, to name but a few, God was opening the windows of Heaven and pouring out His Blessing.

The Trawler Bus Ministry was in operation after much hard work by many different people to whom we are deeply indebted. What a joy and privilege it was to have people come on board the bus, people from dysfunctional families and broken marriages, abused wives, depressed men, so many who were without hope, and to give them food parcels, wash bags, blankets, clothes and, primarily, tell them about the love of Christ, a real hope that they could discover and experience.

One story that I will share with you which took place on the streets of Edinburgh is about two brothers we met within a few

yards of each other, Kenny and Andy. My little son Luke has got
a massive heart of compassion, so we went to McDonalds and
purchased two bags of the burgers that cost ninety nine pence
each. Off we set around the streets of Edinburgh sharing the love
of Christ over a hamburger or cheeseburger and it was here we
met these two brothers. Broken families, orphans from a young
age and the streets were where they called home, drugs and booze
had taken a toll on these two lovely men, sin had ravished havoc
in their lives, it was written all over their faces, only the love
of Christ could rescue these men. We sat on the bridge beside
them as they each devoured a burger and asked for one for later
that was placed with care into their pockets, we told them about
the love of Christ and they bowed their heads on the street and
prayed the sinner's prayer.

I dared to believe that God was preparing my heart once again,
this was where I felt the need was, sharing the gospel with
people who society and, ashamedly, the church of Jesus Christ
had neglected, these were the people that needed to hear it. As a
family we began to seek earnestly where God would have us to
be used most effectively for His kingdom. Church can become at
times so ritualistic, things have to be carried out at a certain time
and in a certain way and all too often the freedom and liberty that
we should be enjoying in the Spirit just is not there. The reason
being of course, that there is no room or time within the formats
of our services to allow the Holy Spirit in. Vance Havner said, "So
many churches start at 11am sharp but end at 12 noon blunt."

We had developed a praying council of friends around us who
only God could have brought into our lives, they were adamant
that God was going to stir up our hearts to step out in faith and
do the 'work of an evangelist'. We loved the church we were
pastoring in, we loved every single believer so much, they were
our family, the kids in the fellowship we loved, God was blessing
and we wanted to stay, but we had promised the Lord, that if He
opened the door we had to walk through. *I know your deeds.*
See, I have placed before you an open door that no one can

shut. I know that you have a little strength, yet you have kept my word and have not denied my name (Revelation 3:8).

So it was that on Sunday 24th May 2012, my dear friend and brother in the Lord Raymond McDowell brought a message from the Lord to me and to the people of Dunseverick Baptist:

The prophet that hath a dream, let him tell a dream; and he that hath my word, let him speak my word faithfully. What is the chaff to the wheat? Saith the Lord. Is not my word like as a fire? saith the Lord and like a hammer that breaketh the rock in pieces? (Jeremiah23:28-29)

Fear not my son. Fear not when you declare my truth. Tremble not at their faces when they set themselves against you. It is not you that they reject, it is me that they reject, so tremble not at them, but rather tremble at my coming judgement upon those who have believed not. For I am a righteous God and shall not I judge righteously?

I have given you many counsellors over the years and you have willingly sat at their feet and taken counsel as from Me saith the Lord. You have studied to show thyself approved, not unto men, but unto God, a workman that needeth not to be ashamed, rightly dividing the word of truth. Moreover you have listened to the counsel of the Holy Spirit and obeyed His leading, and in that you have delighted my heart. I have much more to teach you my son in the ways of the Spirit. I have looked into your heart and I see a reflection of my own heart to the lost. It can be truly said of you as was spoken of my servant King David, "that he was a man after mine own heart."

Patience my son. You will not always minister to this people here as their pastor because I have other work for you in many places and will expand your ministry. But neither you nor this people are to be sad when you leave this place because you will leave a people more spiritually astute and willing to walk in recognition and obedience to His leading.

So my son, declare my word faithfully, for what is the chaff to the wheat?

Those who have ears to hear let them hear what the Spirit is saying, saith the Lord your God in the midst.

I was humbled beyond comprehension, here was a Godly man who I looked up to, a brother that I had come to love and trust and God had given him a message to share with me.

After this message I prayed the more earnestly, it was a simple prayer, not full of high and mighty strung phrases or big theological expressions, it was simply this, "Lord teach me to fish."

Yes, I was engaged in gospel preaching and missions, but was I as Paul encouraged young Timothy making full proof of my ministry? I wanted to be a bondservant, a labourer, a soul winner, not a pulpit filling pastor, I longed for God to teach me more of Himself and His character in the Spirit of truth.

I gave myself to prayer and the Word of God and I was truly blessed as God revealed Himself and His plans for my life and our family through His word.

Let us take yet another Selah and let me share what God gave me through Nehemiah 4 vs.1-23. Again we take this story as recorded for us in the King James Version of scripture.

When Nehemiah turned up in Jerusalem it seems so clear that Sanballat saw him as a real threat, Sanballat was very happy with a weakened Jewish people and they were dependant on him, if Nehemiah was going to have an impact then Sanballat knew that the Jews would get stronger and Jerusalem would get stronger and this would have serious repercussions on his stronghold on the situation.

The context of this passage that I have suggested to you brings us into a project that Nehemiah and his men are involved in, this project is a very critical and an important one, the bottom line is, that the future of Jerusalem and of Israel itself will depend on how successful these men are and if they complete the project assigned to them. Time and time again I have come back to the book of Nehemiah, time and time again I have came back to this very chapter. Can I say, as you will already know, when the work is going well be prepared for trouble, the enemy does not want to see the work of the Lord being successful in any way. It is very obvious that when we are content with the norm of life the enemy will be happy and leave us alone but when you want to step out and do something for God just you watch and see how the enemy strikes, it happened in Nehemiah's day and I can assure you that it is no different today.

When you read from Nehemiah chapter four through to chapter six you will notice that, at the very minimum, there are nine different tactics which the enemy uses to try and stop the work going on. The attacks are divided into two, at first the enemy tries to attack the workers, the Jewish people themselves and when he sees that fail in chapter six, then the attention turns to the leader himself Nehemiah. But not one of the tactics that were tried in order to disrupt the work succeeded, Nehemiah stood strong and thank God the work was finished in fifty two days.

If you want to be a builder then you have to be a battler!!

I trust and pray as we go through this chapter together that you and I will both learn that there is work to be done, there is to be no slacking. How sad it is that so many evangelical believers have become comfortable with just the norm and yet the Word of God is so potently clear, *As long as it is day, we must do the work of him who sent me. Night is coming, when no one can work (John 9:4).*

- IDENTIFY THE PITFALLS - Nehemiah chapter 4

As I read through this chapter there were a few pitfalls that became very apparent, let me just highlight three of them:

(i) **D**isapproval vs.1-3 - Criticism is an awful thing, that well known writer Shakespeare said of criticism, "it is paper bullets of the brain," but how sadly too often those bullets of verbal ammunition have taken out many labourers in the work of the Lord, many people can stand strong when shot at but can easily fall when laughed at. In vs.2 Sanballat calls the Jews **"feeble"** that word really means **"withered or miserable."** To begin with Sanballat shows his disapproval in the direction of the workers, what he saw from the human eye, was a few feeble people trying to do a mammoth job, but what he did not see was a mammoth God who was using the feeble workers. Never forget who God chooses for His work, *But God chose the foolish things of the world to shame the wise; God chose the weak things of the world to shame the strong. He chose the lowly things of this world and the despised things – and the things that are not – to nullify the things that are, so that no one may boast before him (1Corinthians 1:27 -29).* How true, it is so often that workers face disapproval, you always get those that will do it better, or do it differently, generally those are the people that will end up not doing it at all.

But then the disapproval moves from the workers to the actual work itself, look at the four questions that Sanballat asks, "Will they fortify themselves?" in other words he is laughing at them and really saying "How can these weaklings build something strong enough to save them from attack?" Then he poses the next question, "Will they sacrifice?" In other words he is laughing again and saying, "It will take more than prayer to build the walls," what an insult to Jehovah God, next he asks, "Will they finish in a day?" implying again, in laughter, that the feeble workers did not know the size of the task and would soon throw in the towel. Finally he asks about the stones, Sanballat believes that the stones are nothing more than rubbish, sure they had been destroyed and would never stand the test now. Sanbbalat is slightly confused in this respect because, yes there is no question about it that fire would soften the limestone, but look what it says in vs.13 of Nehemiah chapter 2, *And I went out by night by the gate of the valley, even before the dragon well, and to the dung port, and viewed the walls of Jerusalem, which were broken down, and the gates thereof were consumed with fire.*

The walls were broken down and it was the gates that were consumed with fire, there were still plenty of great stones with which to build. You notice in vs.3 that Sanballat has someone with him to help in his accusations of disapproval, Tobiah the Ammonite. He was there at the inspection of the Samaritan army and he joined in disapproval with a laugh saying, "It wouldn't take an army to throw down these walls, a wee fox could do it." Do you every notice that when there is disapproval there are generally a couple of families in on it. A few wee phone calls to rally support and then it is the case of coming together to disapprove.

(ii) **D**evising vs.7-8 – There are four different groups mentioned in vs.7. The city is now completely surrounded, up North was Sanballat and the Samaritans, out East was Tobiah and the Ammonites, down South was Geshem and the Arabs, and out West were The Ashdodites. Significantly too, Asdod was, in all probability, the most important city in Philistia at this time so you can imagine the interest that the Philistines had in the building work going on. And here are these four armies devising together against the people of God,

I always notice how the enemies of God generally unite against the people of God and how very often the people of God generally do not unite against the enemies of God. Please always remember we are in a battle that is outside of the churches four walls, *Jesus knew their thoughts and said to them, "Every kingdom divided against itself will not stand (Matthew 12:25).*

(iii) **D**iscouragement vs.10-12 – It is normal to expect an attack from the world but when it comes from within the church and believers, it is a whole different ball game. If ever there is one successful thing that the enemy will use against the people of God it is discouragement. When we take our eyes off the person, Christ, and start to focus on the problems, then spiritually we are in decline, it is only too apparent when the focus shifts that discouragement will set in and the people of God will become weak. Interesting to note that the discouragement came about from the tribe of Judah, imagine that tribe with David's royal blood running through them and yet they are the ones here that cause the discouragement. Do you know why? One single thing, Compromise. If you were to read in Nehemiah chapter 6 vs.17-19 you will see that some of the tribe of Judah were actually compromising secretly with the enemy, they had married into them, something which God had forbidden, they were more interested in making a wee bit of money out of their collusion with the enemy than standing with God's people. The exact same thing is happening in the work today, there are generally more discouragers than encouragers. Why is it today that sadly in many cases there is very little difference between a 'professing Christian' and an unbeliever? Compromise! An enticing tool of Satan to hinder a Christian to be absolutely surrendered to Christ and the work of the kingdom. So many messages are preached about 'Lukewarm Christianity' but the reality is that we are somehow enjoying this kind of Christianity. 'Lukewarm

Christianity' and compromise do not sit well with God. There seems to be a mindset amongst Christians that numbers matter to God, yet the biblical principle is very clear, *"Enter through the narrow gate. For wide is the gate and broad is the road that leads to destruction, and many enter through it. But small is the gate and narrow the road that leads to life, and only a few find it" (Matthew 7:13-14).* Thank God we still have the odd Nehemiah about. Here is what happens in a church where Christ is present:

A church that has passion is a church where "Discouraged folks cheer up, dishonest folks fees up, sour folks sweeten up, closed folk, open up, gossipers shut up, conflicted folks make up, sleeping folks wake up, lukewarm folk, fire up, dry bones shake up, and pew potatoes stand up! But most of all, Christ the Saviour of the entire world is lifted up."

- **INDULGE IN PRAYER** – I love to read how Nehemiah reacted to all the pitfalls, he got down to prayer! Notice who it was that indulged in prayer in Nehemiah chapter 2:

(i) The **O**verseers Prayed vs.4-5 – Very important to notice that the first people to indulge in prayer were those who had the job of overseeing the people. Nehemiah gets straight down to prayer, note that he is not praying for the good of himself, he is praying for the glory of God. What we need in our church fellowships today are good overseers, men of prayer, men who understand that when the going gets tough the tough get going.

(ii) Then **O**thers Prayed vs.9 – You get the pattern here? When the overseers laid by example then others soon followed. If ever there was a day when we needed to be united in prayer it is today. *Pray continually (1 Thessalonians 5:17).*

- ## INVOLVE A PARTNERSHIP

Let me say that prayer is the key foundation to any work of the Lord, but let me also point out from Nehemiah chapter 2 that with prayer there has got to come some work also. Can I just point out to you the partnerships that were formed here were on the basis of prayer:

(i) Partners In The **W**ork vs.6 – I love the two words that are used **"we"** and **"mind"** in vs.6, you know what it really means "that all the people had their heart in the work." Can I be practical and say that the work that we are involved in is not our own work but the Lord's. the harsh reality is that within so many of our church fellowships we have 'kingdom building' taking place, there are those and they feel the Sunday School work is 'their work', the youth is 'their work', the small group is 'their work' and slowly the body of Christ becomes disjointed because we fail to realise that it is the 'Lord's work'. We should be honoured and humbled to appreciate that the Lord chooses to use us in His work, so often we feel that The Lord is the one who should feel honoured that we are helping Him. When our heart is in the work and when we are partners together in the work then greater results will be accomplished. Paul instructed us, *Whatever happens, conduct yourselves in a manner worthy of the gospel of Christ. Then, whether I come and see you or only hear about you in my absence, I will know that you stand firm in one spirit, contending as one man for the faith of the gospel (Philippians 1:27).*

(ii) Partners In the **W**atching vs.9 – It is very apparent that as they worked they watched and they watched both day and night. You see each individual has an eye on the workman beside them, at any moment an attack could have potentially come from any direction, so they were all partners together watching. So many times we are watching to catch our fellow workers out rather than watching to carry our fellow workers along.

(iii) Partners in **W**itness vs.13-18 – I love reading verse 15. How must the enemies have felt when they saw the work coming together, when they saw the unity among the people armed, working and watching? What a witness it must have been of a great God in Israel. You will be aware that everyone "returned unto his own work," they all had different roles, some were sifting through the debris for good materials, others were building, others were cutting, some were carving but one thing they all were doing was praying. All of our roles are different within the building of the church but we cannot do without each other; all of us must have our heart in the work.

One of the greatest mysteries in aerodynamics was why the geese fly in a V –shaped formation. Two engineers undertook the task in a wind tunnel to find out and the discovery was amazing. Each goose in flapping its wings, creates an upward lift for the goose that is following so when each goose carries out its role in the V formation the whole flock has a 71% greater flying range than they would have if they were flying solo. If one goose starts to flag or lag behind something remarkable happens the other geese 'honk' until it gets back in the formation. Can we learn from this? When we fly together in the witness of the work of the Lord I believe that we would have far more than a 71% chance of reaching our goals in our Christian life and if one fellow Christian was to lag behind can we 'honk' them back into formation rather than hound them out of the work all together?

- ## INCORPORATE THE PROSPECTS

  (i) The Prospect Of Their **L**ord – Look at the key phrase
  in vs.14, "remember the Lord" remember **"Adonay"**,
  pronounced **"Ad-o-nay,"** the use of this word stresses the
  emphatic nature of who they were to remember. The Lord
  is referred to here as **"great and awesome."** We should
  always keep this one prospect in view and incorporate it
  into our work, "remember the Lord", remember the Lord
  the next time you are thinking of saying I quit, remember
  the Lord the next time you face criticism, remember the
  Lord the next time you are going to criticise, oh that we
  would just remember the Lord.

  (ii) The Prospect Of Their **L**oved Ones – Nehemiah brings
  to their minds that the very survival of their loved ones
  depends on their work, here is the crux of what the work
  that we are involved in is all about, how we build, how we
  pray, how we watch will have a huge impact on our loved
  ones. It is important that we grasp these two prospects,
  remember the Lord, remember your loved ones.

  ***And let us consider how we may spur one another on
  toward love and good deeds. Let us not give up meeting
  together, as some are in the habit of doing, but let us
  encourage one another – and all the more as you see the
  Day approaching (Heb 10:24 -25).***

  Maybe you feel that there is too much focus on Nehemiah
  and not enough focus on others, so often that can be the case.
  When God raises an individual up with a special anointing to
  carry out a task, other people feel left out and think the focus
  should be on them so they become disgruntled, jealous and
  bitter and try to stifle the work and the servant of the Lord.

  You may recall the story of the elders of a church, meeting
  to discuss who would come to take a Gospel Campaign and

it was agreed that D.L. Moody would be the man to take it. One elder piped up and said, "Does Moody have the monopoly on the Holy spirit?" to which the reply came, "No the Holy Spirit has the monopoly on Moody." Thank God when the Holy Spirit comes upon a person, as the case with D.L Moody, Nehemiah and many other individuals they become mighty tools in the hands of a mighty God. Do not be the one that tries to spoil the workman or the work.

God was preparing my heart, I knew it, I could sense it but what was it that He was going to do? I will never forget the word that was delivered by Raymond from God, I never forgot the message I received and lessons learnt from Nehemiah. The key word was 'Patience', I needed it, this next move had to be of God and it had to come crystal clear and so we as a family did what we always do, we sought the Lord for guidance.

Jehovah, the God of Abraham, Isaac and Jacob, the Covenant God, the God that raised up a man like Nehemiah and a few feeble workers in the eyes of the world, we desperately need You, we thank You for past blessings, but they do not suffice for the present, we claim the victory in a resurrected Christ, we leave our future with You, knowing that You already have it worked out and planned, reveal it to us in Your time, in Jesus name, Amen.

CHAPTER TEN

BEAUTIFUL

Song of Solomon 5:16 His mouth is sweetness itself, he is altogether lovely. This is my lover, this is my friend, O daughters of Jerusalem.

The journey to the Promised Land was to be one of mountains and valleys as we read, *But the land you are crossing the Jordan to take possession of is a land of mountains and valleys that drinks rain from heaven (Deuteronomy 11:11).* It is the exact same in the Christian life, God never promised us a bed of roses, in fact what He promised was a cross, *Then he said to them all: "If anyone would come after me, he must deny himself and take up his cross daily and follow me" (Luke 9:23).* Too many professing Christians are Cross Gazers instead of Cross Carriers. The reality of the Christian life is this, the Lord never wanted Quantity, He only ever wanted Quality, that is the very reason He made this statement. You see, the crowds were following Him in their thousands, they thought this man was just amazing, healing the sick, giving sight to the blind, casting out demons, even raising people from the dead, all of the people wanted in on the action. This is no different today, when people hear or see something wonderful happening in a particular church it attracts crowds. But yet, the reality that Jesus Christ spoke about was the opposite of crowd drawing, it was about crowd thinning. So as Jesus looked and saw the crowds He knew the first thing that would separate the counterfeit followers from the real followers was the use of the word **"stauros"** pronounced **" stow-ros"** which in our English translation is the word **"cross."** The cross to people in Jesus' day was a torture tool used by the Romans, it meant pain, suffering and even death. Were the people that followed Christ ready for that? Scripture gives a clear answer to that, *From this time many of his disciples turned back and no longer followed him. "You do not want to leave too, do you?" Jesus asked the Twelve (John 6:66-67).* The cross has been and will always be the dividing factor in time and in eternity, eternity past knew of no other future than the cross, eternity future will know of no other past than the cross. What does the cross mean to you?

For too long I had lived my Christian life as some kind of fun loving fantasy adventure, I was a 'Christian', but I certainly was not a disciple, it was reality I was searching for, it was desperation to know God. Paul got it right when he wrote, *But whatever was to my profit I now consider loss for the sake of Christ. What is more, I consider everything a loss compared to the surpassing greatness of knowing Christ Jesus my Lord, for whose sake I have lost all things. I consider them rubbish, that I may gain Christ and be found in him, not having a righteousness of my own that comes from the law, but that which is through faith in Christ – the righteousness that comes from God and is by faith. I want to know Christ and the power of his resurrection and the fellowship of sharing in his sufferings, becoming like him in his death, and so, somehow, to attain to the resurrection from the dead. Not that I have already obtained all this, or have already been made perfect, but I press on to take hold of that for which Christ Jesus took hold of me (Philippians 3:7-12).*

The more of the beauty I saw in Christ, the more of His holiness I saw in the Word of God, it was only then the more real that the Christian life seemed to become. As Heather and I sat one evening in our devotional time we had just finished reading the following verses, *"The land we passed through and explored is exceedingly good. If the Lord is pleased with us, he will lead us into that land, a land flowing with milk and honey, and will give it to us. Only do not rebel against the Lord, and do not be afraid of the people of the land, because we will swallow them up. Their protection is gone, but the Lord is with us. Do not be afraid of them"* (**Numbers 14:7-9**). As we ended the reading of these verses the time approached 11:20pm, as Heather pulled the blinds to go off to bed, the key words that were coming to us both with power were, "only do not rebel against the Lord." I plugged my mobile phone into the charger and, as I did so, a message came through and here is what it said, "Hi, the way is beginning to be made clear. Joshua chp.1 – Blessings N."

Our dear friend Norman Lynas, a man with passion for the gospel of Jesus Christ, a man with a hunger to see not just 'believers' but 'followers' someone that I had been meeting for many years of my life to glean wisdom, direction and accountability, and he sends this text to us just at Gods appointed timing. I felt the warmth of the very presence of the Holy Spirit flood my entire body. Norman Lynas, a man, who with his wife Lynda had stepped out in faith many years previous and had set off on a journey to provide young people an opportunity to develop their Christian walk, a venue in which they could come and experience 'discipleship' and begin this remarkable journey of being 'Christ followers'. Norman knew what it meant to 'put feet to faith' and so 'Exodus' was formed and to this very day hundreds of young people continue to meet and experience mentoring and many go to various countries around the world to share the love of Jesus Christ.

Confirmation!!! We heard God, we were to step out into this vast harvest field in faith. Now was the time, there was to be no delay and so with a humble gratitude in our hearts and excitement welling up within us, with much prayer and many Bible readings it was made clear to us that, 'Christ In You Evangelistic Association' was to be commenced. This ministry would have the vision to reach out with the gospel of Jesus Christ, to see many people becoming followers of Him but not just leaving new believers to grope and grapple in their new Christian life but to encourage them to become disciples and evangelists, so that they too can become soul winners.

It was with sadness and excitement that we met with the church fellowship of Dunseverick Baptist Tabernacle to tell them the news. They understood, they knew God was working in our lives, and it was with their blessing that we were to go and share the love of the Lord Jesus Christ with others. How we thank God for so many wonderful people in Dunseverick Baptist, there are many within that little fellowship that long to see God move in the power of the Holy Spirit. We as a family will continually be remembering in prayer the work and ministry of this church.

It would be good to have a Selah here and to focus on Christ, because He is the centre, the Pre-eminent One, *And he is the head of the body, the church; he is the beginning and the firstborn from among the dead, so that in everything he might have the supremacy (Colossians 1:18).*

I would love to share with you something special that God through the Holy Spirit shared to me, it is my heart's desire that you see no one other than God and the glory of God as you read this book.

Isaiah, what a man he was, his name means **"Jehovah is helper or salvation is of the Lord,"** he was married to a prophetess and she bore him two sons, whose names were, **Shear-jashub** which means **"a remnant shall return"** and **Maher-shalal-hash-baz** which means **"make haste."** Isaiah was very patriotic he loved his nation but most importantly he loved his God. Isaiah ministered during the reign of King Uzziah. What a man he was, he described God so often as "The Holy One Of Israel." Of course many of us lift out verses that we love from his writings and no chapter is more read than Isaiah chapter 53, but chapter 6 stands out for me so much as I read through this wonderful book. We refer once more to this passage as recorded in the King James Version.

There is a challenge for us all from chapter six, I pray it will speak to your heart as it spoke to mine.

- A SOBERING CRISIS - vs.1a –

Look at the way the chapter starts, "in the year that King Uzziah died." Uzziah was the 10th king in Judah and what a Godly king he was. Zechariah had a huge influence on his life and out of all the kings, Uzziah never totally departed from following the Lord, although you will read in 2nd Chronicles 26 vs.16 that he made the mistake of offering incense in the temple and because of this he was stricken with leprosy and he lived with that condition from that moment until his death. The sobering crisis is this, Uzziah was king for 52 years and during this time the Southern Kingdom had enjoyed wealth and success such as had not been seen since the reign of Solomon. Going on past experiences when a Godly leader died, generally the people returned to pagan worship and so Isaiah felt that this meant crisis time could just be around the corner. What I love is that in a time when Isaiah could have lost focus and could have got down under it, he redirected his attention and focus on the Lord and he got a fresh glimpse of God's glory. Are there not times in all of our lives when we face the sobering crisis of death and we seem to lose the focus? Are there not times in all of our lives when we feel that after a crisis a downfall is just waiting, looming large around the corner for us? What we need is what Isaiah witnessed, we need what takes place in the next few verses.

- A SOVEREIGN CONSECRATED – vs.1b-4

Look at where the Lord is sitting, "on the throne," we sing it so often,

**Have you started for glory and Heaven?
Have you left this old world far behind?
In your heart is the Comforter dwelling?
Can you say, "Praise the Lord, He is mine"?
Have the ones that once walked on the highway**

Gone back, and you seem all alone?
Keep your eyes on the prize, for the home in the skies;
God is still on the throne.

God is still on the throne,
And He will remember His own;
Tho' trials may press us and burdens distress us,
He never will leave us alone;
God is still on the throne,
He never forsaketh His own;
His promise is true, He will not forget you,
God is still on the throne.

But do we really believe that? An earthly king had died but the Heavenly King was still on the throne, I have a little quote in my study that says, "When the outlook looks grim, try the uplook." Isaiah says, "I saw the Lord," so he saw the Lord and actually lived? This is some shouting material right here! Isaiah did see the Lord and yes he did live! The fear that gripped the Old Testament believers that if they saw the Lord they would die, well that fear is completely obliterated here. There is a relaxed sort of attitude that is creeping in among many believers in relation to who God is and the relationship that we are to have with Him. Warren Wiersbe, in his book on True Worship, says, "We must beware of trying to get chummy with God. I know the apostle John leaned on the bosom of Jesus in the Upper Room; but he fell at the feet of Jesus when he beheld Him in His sovereign glory (Revelation 1:17)." Then Wiersbe continues, "There is an undue familiarity with God that only proves that the worshipper does not really know God at all" (Warren Wiersbe, True Worship, p.26).

In Isaiah 6 we have the only mention in scripture of seraphim, the highest order of angel, the Hebrew word is **"seraph,"** pronounced **"saw-rawf,"** it literally means **"to burn,"** this is in relation to the holiness of God, but look at what they are doing they are covering their faces with their wings, they understood that they were in the presence of holiness and they covered themselves, and cried, *"Holy, holy, holy, is the LORD of hosts: the whole earth is full of his glory."* The fact that they echo the word "holy" three times is hugely significant in Jewish culture as it impresses the completeness and uniqueness of the holiness of God. The house was filled with smoke, a symbol of the very presence of God and His train filled the temple showing us that the whole setting and central theme is God and His holiness. I hope that we understand this, the main attribute of our sovereign God today is holiness, and you and I must live holy lives before Him because He is holy. *"Consecrate yourselves and be holy, because I am the Lord your God (Leviticus 20:7).* From a Heavenly point of view, the "whole earth was filled with His glory."

- A **S**INFUL **C**ONDITION VS.5-7 -

A sure sign of a spiritual person who has sensed the holiness of God and got a glimpse of it is that they will sense something else of importance and that is, the sinful condition of themselves. Look at Isaiah, he does not cry, "Woe is that man over there," "Woe is that brother," he cries "Woe is me." Dear believer, you and I will never be anything if we never get a glimpse of what we are, you see unclean lips are brought about by an unclean heart, *The good man brings good things out of the good stored up in him, and the evil man brings evil things out of the evil stored up in him. But I tell you that men will have to give account on the day of judgement for every carless word they have spoken (Matthew 12:35-36).*

- A SATISFYING CURE - VS.6&7 –

Isaiah needs something and David needed it too as you read his words, *Create in me a pure heart, O God, and renew a steadfast spirit within me (Psalm 51:10).* They both needed cleansed and it needed to be an inward cleansing. This scene is in Heaven, but had it been on earth then the coals would have been taken off the brazen altar where the sacrificial blood had been shed, or even possibly from the censer of the high priest on the day of atonement, either way there had to be blood for the cleansing. But this is an angel with a live coal of fire from the altar in Heaven, the closer you get to the Lord the worse you will look but there is cleansing. Oh that the coals of fire might touch your lips, that you and I might experience a real cleansing afresh. The only people that God can use and will use are these, *Who may ascend the hill of the Lord? Who may stand in his holy place? He who has clean hands and a pure heart, who does not lift up his soul to an idol or swear by what is false (Psalm 24:3).* As I type this verse right now the magnitude of what I have just typed has gripped me. Just this year I have been reminded so much of my own weakness and personal sin, to think that you cannot fall or be caught up in sin is nothing more than a lie that God hates, pride. How do I know? Because I fell! David's cry comes to me with a freshness just now, *"How the mighty have fallen!" (2nd Samuel 1:19).*

- A SINCERE CALL VS.8

What a call, *Also I heard the voice of the Lord, saying, Whom shall I send, and who will go for us? (Isaiah 6:8).* What the nation needed was the Lord and what the Lord needed was a servant to go, nothing has changed even in our modern day, in fact if ever there was to be a more earnest and impressive need for a nation to receive the Lord and have someone to go tell them about the Lord, it is definitely today. This nation still needs the Lord and the Lord still needs people to go. There is verse that I so often read which speaks of the sins of Jerusalem and what will befall them, *"I looked for a man among them who would build up the wall and stand before me in the gap on behalf of the land so I would not have to destroy it, but I found none (Ezekiel 22:30).* There is a very distinct pattern here, we have to see the holiness of God, then we have to see the sinfulness of ourselves and when we get this Biblical pattern right then we will see the state of the world and the need around us. There is absolutely no point in sitting in little 'holy huddles' and praying week after week, year after year, "Lord, bring sinners in" the Word of God is clear we as believers have to "Go," the challenge is still the same as John records, *Do you not say, 'Four months more and then harvest'? I tell you, open your eyes and look at the fields! They are ripe for harvest (John 4:35).*

- A SELFLESS CONCLUSION VS.8 –

With so many of the people in the Bible, when they got the call from the Lord they would have done well as politicians, especially here in Northern Ireland because they began discussions on the matter, but not so with Isaiah here was his answer, *"Then said I, Here am I; send me."* We hear it so often, God is not interested in our ability He is only interested in our availability. Sadly the problem today and the reason why there are so few labourers and such ineffective soul winning, is that we have never got a glimpse of His glory in order to be in a position to be used.

I am not sure if you are aware how the Welsh Revival came about but let me share with you how. During the spring of 1904 a young Welshman named Evan Roberts, having been repeatedly wakened at 1:00am, and meeting with God from 1am until 5am, discovered and got a real glimpse of the holiness of God. The churches increasingly became packed and prayer rooms could hardly contain the people. Pastor Joseph Jenkins asked for testimonies, a young fifteen year old girl, named Florrie Evans, stood up and said these few words, "I love Jesus with all my heart." She had been saved only a few days but with these few words the whole atmosphere of the meeting changed, a sense of the Spirit of God was felt and, as a consequence of the public confession by a young girl over one hundred thousand people came to know the Saviour

Two modern singer/songwriters who originally came from Northern Ireland are Keith & Kristyn Getty. I love this song, it challenges my heart, may it challenge yours:

HEAR THE CALL OF THE KINGDOM
**Lift your eyes to the King
Let His song rise within you
As a fragrant offering
Of how God rich in mercy
Came in Christ to redeem
All who trust in His unfailing grace**

Hear the call of the Kingdom
To be children of light
With the mercy of heaven
The humility of Christ
Walking justly before Him
Loving all that is right
That the life of Christ may shine through us

King of Heaven we will answer the call
We will follow bringing hope to the world
Filled with passion filled with power to proclaim
Salvation in Jesus' name

Hear the call of the Kingdom
To reach out to the lost
With the Father's compassion
In the wonder of the cross
Bringing peace and forgiveness
And a hope yet to come
Let the nations put their trust in Him

Are you ready to get a glimpse and see the Lord?

Father, I thank You for getting a glimpse of Your glory, I thank You for understanding something of who You are and what I am, I want to hear the call of God clearly in my life, I am willing to go where you may lead. Must I be carried to the skies on flowery beds of ease, while others fought to win the prize and sailed through bloody seas, make me uncomfortable Lord with the norm, lead me into higher plans, thank You for the cross, the resurrection and the truth that Christ lives in me. We bless Your Holy name, for Christ' sake, Amen.

CHAPTER ELEVEN

BEYOND..........

Lu 13:34 "O Jerusalem, Jerusalem, you who kill prophets and stone those sent to you, how often I have longed to gather your children together, as a hen gathers her chicks under her wings, but you were not willing!

I had felt that there was not another chapter to be compiled for this book, but from the commencement of 2013 there has been a huge burden upon me for the town in which I am so privileged to now live. For so many people Bushmills is only a tourist attraction with great coffee shops, chip shops and hotels and of course beautiful scenery, especially that of the world famous Giant's Causeway, but now that I have been resident in Bushmills it is so much more to me. What in fact makes Bushmills the place that it is, are the people who live here all the year around. I have grown to know and love so many people in this town, their kindness, humbleness and their deep sense of appreciation when any act of kindness is shown to them is something that has humbled me and made me value and appreciate the compassion that the Lord Jesus Christ has for mankind.

Since my arrival in Bushmills in 2009 I have been genuinely moved and overwhelmed by the number of sudden deaths in the district. I am convinced in my heart that God is speaking and moving in this area, but yet it is a little town with many similarities to other towns and cities, many people seem to have forgotten about God and have lost the realisation that there is an "after this" after death.

During the month of August 2013, we had the unmistakable privilege of erecting a tent in Millennium Park kindly offered to us by Moyle District Council for the crusade entitled 'Revival By The River'. We enjoyed having two anointed servants of the Lord, David Legge and Alan Bartley along to share with us in the preaching of the gospel. After months of planning and prayerful preparation the Revival Crusade commenced and immediately it became apparent that God was moving in the power of the Holy Spirit as hundreds of people availed themselves of the opportunity of the tent being there and came in under the sound of the gospel. Many responded during that week and made commitments to the Lord Jesus Christ, but it was during that week that something momentous took place.

Due to the tragic death of one of the local young men in the district in the middle of the week God moved in a way that I had never observed before in my Christian walk. There were so many young people left devastated and totally bewildered at this sudden death, the question being asked by them was a logical one and one that so many would ask, Why? The old must die, yes, but the young may die. The truth of scripture was made apparent once more, ***Now listen, you say, "today or tomorrow we will go to this or that city, spend a year there, carry on business and, make money." Why you do not even know what will happen tomorrow. What is your life? You are a mist that appears for a little while and then vanishes (James 4:13-14).***

Many of the young people came to the tent and with joy, tears and a sense of the awesomeness of God many of them responded and came to know Jesus Christ as their personal Saviour.

The reality was that God was speaking, but there was lethargy, denial and sadly disinterest with so many, yet these words came so forcibly to my mind, ***If only they were wise and would understand this and discern what their end will be! (Deuteronomy 32:29).***

Before we conclude this book, I would love to leave a challenge, because if you ever meet me and forget me you have lost nothing but if you meet with Christ and forget Him, you have lost everything.

How shall we escape if we ignore such a great salvation? This salvation, which was first announced by the Lord, was confirmed to us by those who heard him (Hebrews2:3).

There was a man by the name of **William Hope** who died in 1797, it is said of William that he was the leader of a group of people who blasphemed God and ridiculed and openly taunted Christians. One of the things that William and his followers did was to openly kick publicly the Bible around a floor and tear it to pieces. Let me take you to the moment of William Hope's death and tell you of the fear and terror that engulfed him as his friends watched and heard what he said as he died: "I have no contrition, I cannot repent. God will damn me, I know that the day of grace is past, you see one who is damned forever, oh eternity, oh eternity, nothing for me now but hell, come eternal torments I hate everything that God has made, only I have no hatred for the devil I wish to be with him, I long to be in hell, can you all not see him, he is coming for me?"

Voltaire - That famous French infidel and one of the most talented writers of his generation, used his writings to demean and try to wreck Christianity. Here is what he said of the Lord Jesus Christ, "curse the wretch" and on another occasion here is what he said, "In twenty years Christianity will be no more, my single hand shall destroy the edifice it took twelve apostles to rear." Shortly after his death, the very house where his blasphemous literature was printed was the depot of the Geneva Bible Society. The nurse who attended Voltaire said, "For all the wealth in Europe I would not see another infidel die." Dr. Trochim who was attending him as he died, said that he cried out most horribly, " I am abandoned by God and man, I will give you half of what I am worth if you will give me six months life, then

I shall go to hell and you will go with me, no Christ, no Jesus Christ"

How sad, two men who left this world with no hope, they chose to ignore and reject so great salvation, when it was just too late these men became fully aware of the reality of God's great eternity. It is heart wrenching to think of those who live and die without salvation and to understand when it is too late that all along this salvation was freely offered and available for them.

Let me share with you some quotes of those who accepted this great Salvation:

D.L Moody – "Earth recedes, heaven opens before me, if this is death, this is sweet, there is no valley here, God is calling me and I must go." His son was standing by his bedside and said, "No father you are dreaming." "No" said Mr. Moody, "I am not dreaming I have been within the gates, I have seen the children's faces." A short time went by, then Mr Moody said these words as he closed his eyes in death, "This is my triumph, this is my coronation day it is glorious."

Matthew Henry – "Sin is bitter, I bless God I have inwards support."

Martin Luther – "Our God is the God from whom cometh salvation, God is the Lord whom we escape death."

John Knox – "Live in Christ, live in Christ and the flesh need not fear death."

John Calvin – "Thou Lord bruisest me, but I am abundantly satisfied since it is from Thy hand."

John Wesley – "The best of all is, God is with us. Farewell Farewell."

Charles Wesley – "I shall be satisfied with thy likeness satisfied, satisfied."

Baxter – "I have pain but I have peace, what a peace."

Treston – "Blessed be God, though I change my place I shall not change my company."

Goodwin – "Ah is this dying? How have I dreaded as an enemy this smiling friend?"

Everette – "Glory, glory, glory" he repeated this for twenty five minutes and it only came to an end when his life ceased.

I want to conclude in reference to how I began, my initial perception of how I viewed people was Protestant and Catholic, there are two classes of people who the Word of God speaks of, it is not Protestant or Catholic, it is not black or white, it is not Muslim or Jew, the Word of God clearly pinpoints only two classes of people, there are those who are saved, born again, converted whatever terminology you would like to use and there are those who are not saved. Only God and you know exactly which division you fall into.

If He is calling you I suggest that you do not ignore Him, there could come a point when He might not speak any more and just like William Hope and Voltaire you will die and go to a Christ rejecter's hell.

Let us look at some reasons as to why Hebrews 2:3 says, "So great salvation." Why is this salvation so great? What is there in it that is so special? –

It is great because of:

1. Its **Ability** –

   This 'so great salvation' can do something that no other plan that has ever been devised can do, it can save a lost sinner,

Paul said, *I thank Christ Jesus our Lord, who has given me strength, that he considered me faithful, appointing me to his service. Even though I was once a blasphemer and a persecutor and a violent man, I was shown mercy because I acted in ignorance and unbelief. The grace of our Lord was poured out on me abundantly, along with the faith and love that are in Christ Jesus. Here is a trustworthy saying that deserves full acceptance: Christ Jesus came into the world to save sinners – of whom I am the worst.*

But for that very reason I was shown mercy so that in me, the worst of sinners, Christ Jesus might display his unlimited patience as an example for those who would believe on him and receive eternal life. Now to the only God, be honor and glory for ever and ever. Amen (1ˢᵗ Timothy 1:12-17). What other message could make such a transformation? I have known drug addicts, prostitutes, alcoholics and murders whose lives have been changed in a moment of time, all because of the ability of this 'so great salvation' take a look around you in the area where you live and I am very sure that you can think of at least one person you know that their life has been changed because of this salvation. This plan of salvation is the only thing that will ever work, there is no other way, no other method, it is salvation by grace alone through faith alone, in Christ alone, *Jesus answered, "I am the way, and the truth and the life. No one comes to the Father except through me" (John 14:6).* I love to read testimonies. What about the man in Mark 5 who dwelt among the tombs and was self harming? Salvation had the ability to change his life forever. What about the woman in John 4 who was involved with all the men? Yet salvation had the ability to change her life forever, this is what she said after her encounter with Christ, *"Come, see a man who told me everything I ever did. Could this be the Christ?" (John4:29).* What about the blind man, in Mark chapter 10?

After he met with Jesus not only had Jesus the power to give him physical sight but, more importantly, spiritual sight as well and here is what it says of him, *"Go," said Jesus, "Your faith has healed you." Immediately he received his sight and followed Jesus along the road (Mark 10:52).* Thank God I believe that this 'so great salvation' has the ability to change *"the vilest offender who truly believes that moment from Jesus a pardon receives."* Do you want real life? Then here is what the Bible says about this salvation and its ability. *The thief comes only to steal and kill and destroy; I have come that they may have life, and have it to the full (John 10:10).*

2. Its Availability –

    The amazing thing about this, 'so great salvation', is that it is available to anyone, anywhere and anytime. Unlike other religions of this world, all of which have rules and regulations and even, in some cases, claim that a person is born into the faith. This salvation is for the, 'whosoever, wherever, whenever'. There are no boundaries to this salvation the Bible says, *in the past God overlooked such ignorance, but now he commands all people everywhere to repent (Acts 17:30). The Lord is not slow in keeping his promise, as some understand slowness. He is patient with you, not wanting anyone to perish, but everyone to come to repentance (2Peter 3:9).* My dear friends you will never be able to blame God if you find yourself lost for all eternity, God has done everything possible for you to be in Heaven.

    It is important to understand that even though this salvation is available to all, there are some things that you must recognize before you come to Christ:

    (i) You have to be a sinner – *For all have sinned and fall short of the glory of God (Romans 3:23).*

(ii) You have to accept that you are a sinner - *When Simon Peter saw this, he fell at Jesus' knees and said, "Go away from me Lord; I am a sinful man!" (Luke 5:8). For I know my transgressions, and my sin is always before me (Ps 51:3).*

(iii) You have to confess your sin - *If we confess our sins, he is faithful and just and will forgive us our sins and purify us from all unrighteousness (1John 1:9).*

(iv) You have to turn from your sin – *I tell you, no! But unless you repent, you too will all perish (Luke 13:3)*

(v) You have to receive the Lord Jesus Christ for salvation – *That if you confess with your mouth, "Jesus is Lord," and believe in your heart that God raised him from the dead, you will be saved. For it is with the heart that you believe and are justified, and it is with your mouth that you confess and are saved (Romans 10:9-11).*

The big problem with people today is that, they do not want to admit that they are sinners. If you never acknowledge that you are a sinner then there is no salvation for you. However the good news about this, 'so great salvation' is that regardless of what you have done in life, it is available to you. *All that the Father gives me will come to me, and whoever comes to me I will never drive away (John 6:37).* It is lovely to know that this salvation is Free, *Come, all you who are thirsty, come to the waters: and you who have no money, come, buy and eat! Come, buy wine and milk without money and without cost (Isa 55:1).* It is also Frank, *"Neither of them had the money to pay back, so he cancelled the debts of both. Now which of them will love him more?" (Lu 7:42)*

2. Its **A**ccountability –

Although there are so many things in life you cannot rely on, you can depend on this 'so great salvation' with all of your heart. Thank God that His promises are forever settled in Heaven. So often when going around so many doors people say to me "I gave that salvation that you are talking about a try and it did not work for me." I can tell you that this salvation is real and if you are genuine about acknowledging that you are a sinner and genuine about repenting from your sin then I have never met a man or woman yet who have genuinely repented of their sin and taken Christ as Saviour and Lord that this salvation has not worked for. So many people are under the impression now that if they are sincere, church going and honest then God will look at them and surely allow them entrance into Heaven. Let us get this clear, God has provided the only way into Heaven through the precious shed blood of His Only Son, the Lord Jesus Christ, on Calvary's cross. There is no other way, the Bible says that you and I must come via the blood-sprinkled way I love that old hymn written by Jessie .B. Pounds,

1. I must needs go home by the way of the cross,
There's no other way but this;
I shall ne'er get sight of the Gates of Light,
If the way of the cross I miss.

• Refrain:
The way of the cross leads home,
The way of the cross leads home;
It is sweet to know, as I onward go,
The way of the cross leads home.

2. I must needs go on in the blood-sprinkled way,
The path that the Saviour trod,
If I ever climb to the heights sublime,
Where the soul is at home with God.

3. Then I bid farewell to the way of the world,
To walk in it nevermore;
For my Lord says, "Come," and I seek my home,
Where He waits at the open door.

There always has to be the Blood, *In fact, the law requires that nearly everything be cleansed with blood, and without the shedding of blood there is no forgiveness (Hebrews 9:22).*

There are four things you need to know that God requires you to understand.

(i) God wants you to know that there is no sin that he does not hate. *Your eyes are too pure to look on evil; you cannot tolerate wrong. (Habakkuk 1:13).* God hates all sin but loves all sinners.

(ii) God wants you to know that there is not one sinner to whom His love does not reach *–But God demonstrates his own love for us in this: While we were still sinners, Christ died for us (Romans 5:8).* God's love is boundless, it reaches high and stoops low.

(iii) God wants you to know that there is no other plan other than salvations plan, *"I tell you the truth, no one can see the kingdom of God unless he is born again" (John 3:3).* Salvation is God's only plan to rescue you and restore you into a relationship with Him that sin has broken.

(iv) God wants you to know that there is no better time for you to be saved than right now - *For he says, "In the time of my favour I heard you, and in the day of salvation I helped you. I tell you, now is the time of God's favour, now is the day of salvation (2nd Corinthians 6:2).* Salvation is only offered to you now, there is no guarantee of tomorrow.

Every other thing will let you down if you are not depending on salvation, salvation is 100% dependable.

3. Its **A**ssure Ability –

I tremble when I hear folk saying that you can lose this
'so great salvation'. Let me tell you about the assure ability
of salvation. I wonder do you ever look at your home and
understand that it will wear out and will not last forever, do
you ever look at your car or your clothes or do you ever stand
and look at your own body and realise that it is in a state of
decay? But there is assurance with salvation! Here are some of
the verses that God's Word lays down which show that this
salvation is a transaction that is eternal:

(i)   It is life everlasting – *For God so loved the world that he
      gave his one and only Son, that whoever believes in him
      shall not perish but have eternal life (John 3:16).*

(ii) It will never allow you to perish – *I give unto them
      eternal life, and they shall never perish; no one can
      snatch them out of my hand (John 10:28).*

(iii) When you come for salvation you will not be refused
      – *All that the Father gives me will come to me, and
      whoever comes to me I will never drive away (John
      6:37).*

(iv) It is salvation that never loses its power – *Therefore he is
      able to save completely those who come to God through
      him, because he always lives to intercede for them
      (Hebrews 7:25).*

(v)   It is a salvation that will save you from wrath to come
      – *Since we have now been justified by his blood, how
      much more shall we be saved from God's wrath through
      him! (Romans 5:9).*

(vi) It is a salvation that promises the Lord's presence with you
      – *Keep your lives free from the love of money and be
      content with what you have, because God said, "Never*

will I leave you; never will I forsake you." (Hebrews 13:5).

4. Its **A**dmire Ability –

This 'so great salvation' oh, there is so much to admire about it, this salvation offers Heaven think about it what other plan can offer anyone Heaven.

Hinduism offers Utopia
Muslims look for Nirvana
Mormonism looks for a world to come
Jehovah's Witnesses look for a Heaven on earth
These are all man's plans and they fail and falter.

Let us just suppose that this 'so great salvation' that is offered to you did nothing more than rescue a soul from hell and take away all of man's sin, you would agree with me that it would be something to admire. But while it is a salvation that will cleanse your sin and will not allow you to be in hell it is also a salvation that promises you a home in Heaven. And wait, this for me is the most admirable thing, it promises that you will be forever in the presence of Christ, and declares the truth that Christ wants to live within you now. *To them God has chosen to make known among the Gentiles the glorious riches of this mystery, which is Christ in you, the hope of glory (Colossians 1:27).*

I am so glad to have the assurance that I am saved, I would not want to be in your place if you are not.

Mr Henry Moorhouse, during his first visit to America in a gospel campaign, was the guest of a very wealthy gentleman who had a daughter who was in her late teens, she was very much looking forward to her wealthy lifestyle and all the parties and popularity that would go with it. One day the young woman came into the library where Mr Moorhouse was reading his Bible, she tried to excuse herself and leave but

Mr Moorhouse looked up and, calling her by her name asked, "Are you saved?" She could only reply, "No Mr Moorhouse, I am not." Then Mr Moorhouse asked, "Would you like to be saved?" The young woman replied, "Yes I would," then came another question from Mr Moorhouse, "Would you like to be saved now?" On being asked that very searching question the young woman thought, she thought of the lifestyle and popularity that she had anticipated but on the other hand she thought of Christ and all that He had done at Calvary for her and then she replied to the question, "Yes Mr Moorhouse I would like to be saved now." Mr Moorhouse took her to Isaiah 53 and asked her to read it. When she had finished he said to her, "Now, read it again and where you read "we" and "our" and "us" please put in "I" and "my" and "me." The young woman started to read and then she came to, "He is despised and rejected of men, a Man of sorrows and acquainted with grief and **I** hid as it were **my** face from Him, He was despised and **I** esteemed Him not, surely He hath borne **my** grief and carried **my** sorrows yet **I** did esteem Him stricken, smitten of God and afflicted, but He was wounded for **my** transgressions, He was bruised for **my** iniquity, the chastisement of **my** peace was laid upon Him and with His stripes **I** am healed." She paused and she looked at Mr Moorhouse and said these words, "Is it true Mr Moorhouse, it was all for me, all for me." Mr Moorhouse replied, "Yes my dear this salvation was all for you."

Are you going to accept, neglect or reject God's wonderful offer of salvation? The choice is entirely yours.

If you would like to come into the good of this salvation, I would invite you to pray the following with me. You must mean this from your heart, the Word of God says, *For with the heart man believeth unto righteousness; and with the mouth confession is made unto salvation (Romans 10:10).* Salvation is a three step process:

1. A - Accept that I am a sinner.

2. B - Believe in your heart that Christ died for your sins, was buried and rose again to give you life.

3. C - Confess with your mouth that Jesus Christ is Lord.

God, thank You for your wonderful plan of salvation, You chose me before the world began and that blows my mind. I understand that to neglect and reject this salvation and to live and die without it offers me no hope, I praise You for the finished work of Christ on the cross, for the blood that He shed, for the sin that he took, it was my sin. I praise You that He was not left in a grave to rot and decay but that He rose again and wants to now impart to me His risen life. I repent of my sins, I ask for the blood of Jesus Christ to cleanse me and to wash me, I ask for forgiveness. I claim this by faith in the name of Jesus. Amen

If for the very first time you have prayed the sinner's prayer from your heart and asked Christ to be your Saviour and Lord of your life, let me take this opportunity to personally welcome you into God's family.

It is important that you tell someone this wonderful life changing news, I would also encourage you to share this news with your pastor or minister or in the case of not being affiliated with a church fellowship make this your first prayer since the sinner's prayer for God to lead you to a fellowship where you will experience love, teaching and nutrition to keep you spiritually healthy.

To help you on your way I would love to share with you some amazing Bible truths, I will give you the references and you can start looking through the Bible for yourself and see just exactly who you are and what you have in Christ now that you are a believer.

In Christ ....

I am **S**atisfied – Justified - Romans 5:1 > Bought - 1st Corinthians
6:19-20 > Adopted - Ephesians 1:5 > Redeemed - Colossians 1:14
> United - 1st Corinthians 6:17 > Member - 1st Corinthians 12:27
> Saint - Ephesians 1:1 > Complete - Colossians 2:10.

I am **S**ignificant – Chosen - John 15:16 > Salt - Matthew 5:13
>Light - Matthew 5:14 > Fruitbearer - John 15:5 > Fellow
Worker - 2nd Corinthians 6:1 > Personal Evangelist - Acts 1:8 >
Minister - 2nd Corinthians 5:17-21 > Temple - 1st Corinthians
3:16 > Strengthened - Philippians 4:13 > God's workmanship -
Ephesians 2:10.

I am **S**ecure - Free from condemnation - Romans 8 :1-2 > Will
never be separated from God's love - Romans 5:35-39 > Sealed by
God - 2nd Corinthians 1 :21-22 > Citizen of Heaven - Philippians
3:20 > Hidden with Christ in God - Colossians 3:3 > Confident
that God will work in me - Philippians 1:6 > Given a Spirit of
power, love and a sound mind - 2nd Timothy 1:7 > I will get grace
and mercy to help when I need it - Hebrews 4:16.

I love this story as a beautiful picture of what the grace of God
can do:

During the late 1800's an English evangelist named Henry
Moorhouse made several trips to preach in America. On one of
those occasions he was taking a walk through a poor section of
town when he noticed a small boy coming out of a store with
a pitcher of milk in his hands. Just then, he slipped and fell
breaking the pitcher and spilling the milk all over the sidewalk.
Mr. Moorhouse rushed to the child's side and found him unhurt
but terrified. "Mu mama'll whip me," he kept crying. So
Mr.Moorhouse picked up the boy and carried him into the
nearby store where the preacher purchased a new pitcher. Then he
returned to the dairy, had the pitcher washed and filled with milk.
With that done, he carried the boy and the pitcher home.

Putting the youngster down on his front porch, Mr. Moorhouse handed him the pitcher and asked, "Will your mama whip you now?"

A wide smile spread across the boys tear stained face, "no sir, cause this is a lot better pitcher than we had before."

In grace God saves us. He doesn't patch up our old lives that have been shattered by sin and Satan into a million pieces. That would not do.

His reputation is at stake. We are His workmanship! He gives us a completely new pitcher .

We would also love to hear from you:

36 Long Commons, Coleraine BT52 1LA
Email: info@ciyea.org.uk
Tel: 028 7032 0062

ACKNOWLEDGEMENTS

Thanks and appreciation to Heather, my wife and main critic, who always keeps me low, tells me to go slow, and never to be a blow and also to Dillon and Luke our two wonderful boys for, their love, patience and forgiveness as I travel sharing with others about 'Christ in you, the hope of glory'. To my two special friends who wish to remain anonymous, the hours that you both spent in reading, correcting and suggesting changes that should be made, my humblest and sincere thanks. To Gwen my secretary, the one that so meticulously endeavours to keep me right, your labour is not in vain. To God, who so graciously picked up broken pieces and with the skill of a Master Builder worked in my life, loving me with a love that is beyond any fragment of my imagination and chose to use me for His Glory alone, I praise Him for that moment in my life when I found this wonderful verse in His word, *A bruised reed he will not break, and a smoldering wick he will not snuff out, till he leads justice to victory (Matthew 12:20).* Thank You for being the God of the second chance, the God of the impossible.

CHRIST IN YOU

EVANGELISTIC ASSOCIATION

Evangelist
Marc Taylor

Focus Five

1 **Visualise**: **John 4:35**
*"Lift up your eyes look at the fields
they are ready to harvest"*

2 **Agonise**: **Thessalonians 5:17**
"Pray and do not cease"

3 **Mobilise**: **Isaiah 6:8**
"Here I am, send me"

4 **Evangelise**: **Mark 16:15**
"Go into all the world and preach the Gospel"

5 **Realise**: **Colossians 1:27**
"Christ in you the hope of glory"

CHRIST IN YOU EVANGELISTIC ASSOCIATION

Inviting people to become followers of Jesus

COUNCIL OF REFERENCE
Rev Hugh Mullan • Roy Walker • Dr Andrew Collins
Rev Jonathan Currie • Val English
Howard Beverland • Canon Norman Porteus
Sam Balmer • David Legge

36 Long Commons, Coleraine BT52 1LA
Email: **info@ciyea.org.uk**
Tel: **028 7032 0062**

If you feel that you would love to contribute to **CIYEA**, it would be most humbly appreciated by Marc, Heather, Dillon and Luke.

As believers, the spreading of The Gospel is dear to all our hearts, so all contributions will go to support Marc and Heather in their endeavour to tell others of Jesus Christ.

❏ I would like to make a

one off payment of £ ....

payable to *'Christ in You Evangelistic Association'*

❏ I would like to make a

monthly/regular payment of £ ....

❏ I am entitled to Gift Aid

Sort Code: 95 06 79
Account No. 5002 1563

Name ....

Address ....

....

Tel: ....